MARKETING HIGH TECHNOLOGY

An Insider's View

William H. Davidow

THE FREE PRESS

THE FREE PRESS
A Division of Simon & Schuster Inc.
1230 Avenue of the Americas
New York, N.Y. 10020

THE FREE PRESS and colophon are trademarks
of Simon & Schuster Inc.

Manufactured in the United States of America

20

Library of Congress Cataloging-in-Publication Data

Davidow, William H.
   Marketing high technology.

   Includes index.
   1. High technology—Marketing.   2. Marketing.
I. Title.
HC79.H53D38   1986   621.381′7′0688   85-28061
ISBN 978-1-4516-9758-2

MARKETING
HIGH
TECHNOLOGY

To Sonja the Perceiver, Carolyn the Creator,
and Becky the Analyzer,
whose support, ideas, and insights have helped so much

Contents

Foreword		*ix*
Acknowledgments		*xiii*
Introduction		*xv*
1.	Crush the Competition	*1*
2.	The Winning Strategy	*12*
3.	Slightly Better Is Dangerous	*37*
4.	Why Companies Give Bad Service	*53*
5.	Great Products Make Great Salespeople	*71*
6.	Great Promotions Are Simple	*89*
7.	Price on Value but Charge What the Market Will Bear	*102*
8.	Be International or Fail	*118*
9.	Plan Products, Not Devices	*133*
10.	Great Products Need a Soul	*147*
11.	Do You Have Marketing?	*157*
12.	The Business of Business Is Total Satisfaction	*171*

Appendix A. The Cost of Attacking a Competitor   179

Appendix B. How Costs and Margin Goals
Affect Price   184

Index   187

Foreword

MANY YEARS AGO, I found myself managing a computer business—the largest, fastest growing, and most profitable division of the Hewlett-Packard Company—and loving the challenge but being frustrated by the brutal competition from my sixteen sister divisions for marketing and other resources. The internal competition made the external competitors DEC and Data General look mild. Being outspoken, I complained at length to Bill Hewlett about the lack of a corporate strategic marketing plan. Some little while later, I found myself assigned to him to solve this exact problem.

While I had been vocal in identifying the problem, when the task became mine I had few ideas on where to begin to solve it. At the beginning, the Boston Consulting Group's newly formulated theories of market share strategy enabled me to tackle effectively the problem I faced, but as I learned in practice, those theories were only a beginning.

In the years since then, the "experience curve," the "cash cow," and the other early theories of market share strategy of BCG have been widely used, more widely abused, and have become a part of business folklore. Good theory is in very short supply in the business world, particularly in marketing, where all too often decisions are made subjectively.

But those market share concepts, while correct (if properly applied), are incomplete. They're similar to Newton's laws of motion, which are valid but cover only limited situations. The genius of Einstein was needed to express adequately a general theory. That's what Bill Davidow has done for marketing in this remarkable book.

Drawing from examples as diverse as a Rolling Stones concert and a microprocessor chip, his definition of a true "product" is both obvious and fundamental. Similarly, ideas for true customer service and the imperative for it are developed. The strategic importance of distribution as it relates to market sector, pricing and the pitfalls it entails, and all the other basics of marketing are analyzed and explained in new ways. These ways build upon the earlier market sector and market share ideas, achieving a synthesis and unity not found elsewhere.

In our era, where devices can be assembled quickly from "product genes" to enter an incredibly crowded market, where simultaneously there can be distribution channel voids and overlaps, where confusion and grid-locked communications are the norm, and where the financial stakes are tremendous, clear new marketing theory is badly needed. Bill Davidow makes this contribution.

I first met the author in the computer wars at Hewlett-Packard, during the time when he was making the transition from Dr. Davidow, computer scientist, to Bill Davidow, sales superstar and topflight marketeer. It is a pleasure now to read this book, which is so rich in personal experience developed in high-tech marketing top management over two decades. But more important, Bill has made a valuable and enduring contribution to the science of marketing.

This is a badly needed contribution, for marketing inefficiency, with all its raminifactions, is appallingly wasteful. Products that fail consume resources in a nonuseful way. There is nothing healthy about competitive death in the market place; both manufacturers and customers lose. What good to anyone is an abandoned home computer gathering dust in the attic? The many "me too" products and even "me too" companies that follow every true innovation don't advance the state of the art; on the contrary, they drain resources from the leaders, rendering everyone more vulnerable to outside competitors such as the wily Japanese. This is true in markets as diverse as semiconductors, genetic engineering, and home entertainment products.

Davidow writes about successful product crusades. Indeed, he is a crusader here, but for all marketing, for all companies: a tough challenge but one handled masterfully. This book should be required reading not only for marketeers, but for all those who depend upon successful new products—from engineers to financiers. I'm glad Bill took the time to make his ideas and insights available to us all.

Thomas J. Perkins
San Francisco

Acknowledgments

THE QUALITY AND READABILITY of this book have been greatly influenced by the efforts of three individuals. Russ Berg, a close friend and a marketing genius, spent a great deal of his time reading and critiquing the manuscript. He contributed a number of valuable ideas. Michael S. Malone edited and helped to rewrite significant portions of the text, making it more readable and immeasurably improving its flow. Bob Wallace, my editor at The Free Press, supported the effort and greatly helped in structuring the manuscript.

All through my life I have been fortunate to have wonderful teachers who have shaped much of my thinking and influenced my actions.

Leonard Davidow, my father, spent much time introducing me to both advertising and promotions.

Theodore Levitt, whom I met first through his articles and books, really is responsible for my selection of marketing as a career and much of my success.

Regis McKenna, a close working associate, taught me a great deal about advertising and public relations.

Tom Perkins, whom everyone thinks of as a venture capitalist, was my first real on-line instructor and a very good one at that.

Franco Mariotti was the first to teach me about international markets.

My friends and associates at Intel have contributed greatly. Andy Grove, its president, really sharpened my management skills, which became a key in marketing successes. If anyone can teach someone how to run a management crusade, he can. Ed Gelbach spent innumerable hours adding reality therapy to my theoretical approaches.

My last staff at Intel were wonderful teachers as well. Tom Kamo and Bernard Giroud added immeasurably to my understanding of international markets. Carlene Ellis and Jim Grenier taught me about service. Frank Gill and Bob Derby contributed greatly to my insights about sales and distribution. Ron Whittier taught me how to make planning in marketing effective. Dick Abascal demonstrated time and time again the value of financial analysis in marketing.

The help and support of those individuals and many others have made this book possible.

Introduction

THE ASCENT OF TECHNOLOGY MARKETING

The mystique of high-technology marketing continues to grow, fed by the spectacular successes of companies like Atari, Lotus Development, and Intel. But insiders see a different picture. Meteoric successes too often turn into overnight disasters. Products sell well for a few weeks, become instant legends, then vanish. With great fanfare corporate giants announce their entry into markets, commit themselves to investing massive resources to gain a leadership position, then stumble, outwitted by nimble start-ups.

Meanwhile, Goliaths stamp out the upstarts in their target markets with seeming ease. Struggles for high-technology market share financed by venture capitalists, corporations, and governments turn into battles of titanic proportion determining the futures of industries and cities, the industrial supremacy of nations.

Apple Computer belittled the late arrival of IBM's merely adequate PC into the personal computer market. Yet within a few months Apple capitulated. Apple's new president, John Sculley, who understood the problem but arrived too late to solve it, admitted that "Apple captured the world's imagination, while IBM captured corporate America's desk tops."

Still later IBM attempted to capitalize on its initial success in the office by extending its dominance into homes and schools with the PC Jr. But the PC Jr. was an instant flop and, after several futile attempts to recuscitate it, died a painful death.

Another example: Visicorp, a company with an insurmountable lead in the spreadsheet software market, vanishes almost overnight, its market position easily captured by another start-up, Lotus. Motorola attacks Intel with an excellent 16-bit microprocessor, the 68000. Both the press and industry gurus proclaim a quick victory for this leadership device. But after a number of years, the 68000 still has managed to capture only a tiny fraction of the 16-bit market. The Intel architecture still owns 85 percent of the market. Meanwhile, Texas Instruments and National Semiconductor, both highly respected for their efficient manufacturing, attack the consumer market with low-cost calculators and watches. Both companies fail miserably in their efforts.

Why are these things happening? Marketing—both good and bad.

TOOTHPASTE TECHNOLOGY

Technology companies are driven continuously to invent and deliver innovations to the market place. But in doing so, they are hampered by the increasing pervasiveness of technological standards. Coerced by the demands of customers, governments, market leaders, and industry standards organizations, they are now increasingly being forced to base their products on identical technologies.

European governments and pan-European organizations are setting standards on communications, teletext, and videotext systems. Consumer companies must conform to identical videotape recording formats. In order to assure themselves of adequate capacity and competitive prices, customers purchasing semiconductors make their suppliers provide them with identical second sources for the products.

Everywhere one looks, forces in the market place are making technology products increasingly homogeneous. More and more products are being built from identical "product genes." With so much in common it has become difficult for the manufacturers to differentiate them in the market place.

The very thought of commodity technology is horrifying to most engineers and technology companies, but they must conform or face abandonment by customers wedded to the benefits and security of standards. They now must find an alternative means to differentiate their products—marketing.

IT'S EASY TO BE HIGH-TECH

At one time it was difficult to develop a new high-tech product. Now it is easy. A few years ago it was an expensive and time-consuming proposition to build a new computer system. Designing the processor and the input/output controllers was costly. Writing the software was laborious, the operating systems and compilers alone requiring tens of worker-years of development.

Today, that same task is comparatively easy. A company need only purchase a standard microprocessor and input/output controllers, then integrate them with standardized operating systems and application packages, and *bingo,* a new computer system.

The result is a proliferation of computer companies and firms building special-purpose computers into their products. That's only one of many revolutions brought on by the advent of commodity technologies. It is now much easier to be a manufacturer of communication systems, electronic watches, high-tech toys, sophisticated defense systems, advanced telephones, electronic switching systems, and so on.

Today there are fewer real trade secrets. The free flow of educated people between companies and countries has made high-tech knowledge available to all. The "cookbooks" of the 1960s that contained much of the black art of making semiconductors are gone forever. The equipment to build the world's most advanced semiconductor products is now commonly available from a number of sources in the United States and Japan. There are a multitude of reliable sources for the high-quality chemicals required to make the intricate processes work.

Thus the semiconductor technology that just a few years ago was the exclusive province of American companies now prospers in Europe, Japan, Taiwan, and Korea. Similar trends are appearing in telephony, genetic engineering, and computing.

Those trends, combined with abundant venture capital, have made it easy to found new technology companies—and easy for established companies to enter high-tech fields. The resulting over-abundance of similar products has led to a series of shakeout wars. Semiconductor companies have vanished, numerous minicomputer and microcomputer companies are gone, and others in many industries will follow.

THE HIGH-TECH HINGE FACTOR

It is easy to be different if there is only one of you. It is much harder to be unique if other companies are doing the same thing with much the same technology. That's what's happening in many high-tech fields. Talk to anyone who has returned from a recent high-tech trade show and you will probably hear: "I was amazed by how so many things looked the same." Pick up an electronics trade journal. The number of companies selling apparently identical products will be overwhelming.

When products appear the same and proliferate to the point where no one can remember their names, marketing becomes a matter of life and death. No customer is going to evaluate ten different word processors or fifty personal computers. Even listing all the alternatives becomes a time-consuming task. So the way he or she feels about the company and the product becomes extremely important. Brand recognition is often decisive.

In the competitive environment, the exposure the product gets through the channels of distribution is critical. If the distributors are confident of the success of a product, they will commit their scarce resources to it.

Needless to say, technological superiority alone no longer guarantees success or even a position in the race. Good devices will not sell themselves. Fortunately for many companies, technological inferiority is not a certain condemnation to failure. Increasingly, marketing will determine the fate of companies.

The environment of the future is one of continually declining product costs driven by the forces of automation, low-cost overseas manufacturing, capital intensity, and increasingly standardized electronics. At the same time the expense of getting the product to the customer and supporting it is going to increase for many products. For a large number, the cost of marketing will soon become the single most important factor in determining the ultimate price a customer must pay. There is no question that the successful technology companies of the future will be market-oriented and marketing-oriented as well as technology-driven.

ABOUT THE BOOK

Much of what is discussed in this book is based on my personal experiences at Intel Corporation. There are two reasons for that. First, they are fresh in my memory. Second, most of the really intelligent things I did in my life I did when I got older. I was a lot smarter when I was young. I knew how things should work and engineered some absolutely brilliant strategic moves. Many of them failed. It was Barney Oliver, the head of Hewlett-Packard Labs, who explained what I was doing wrong. "The only difference," he said, "between theory and practice is that practice takes into account all of the theory." As I got older my theoretical insights were not as brilliant, but things sure worked out better.

It took me years before I discovered that selling the best, the weakest, and the most troubled products all followed remarkably similar patterns. Over time my own actions became more focused, dedicated, and single-minded. Ultimately I came to understand I was not managing or championing products but *crusading* for them, as well as for the customer's interests. The product itself was important, as was the overall marketing strategy, but in the end it was dedication to the product and commitment to the customer that made the difference.

That is the message of this book.

MARKETING HIGH TECHNOLOGY

ONE

Crush the Competition

MARKETING IS CIVILIZED WARFARE. If you find that metaphor too brutal, or if you are not prepared to fight, you should not enlist. As long as aggressive competitors exist—and in this rich and dynamic world they always will—you will be under attack. Your competitors' job is to capture business and then defend that new perimeter. So is yours.

Now, a lot of marketing is creative. It's strategic. Cerebral. But eventually you must make a move—and then the fighting begins. Even the most brilliant campaigns suffer occasional setbacks, and it is during those moments of crisis that the true mettle of the marketing team is tested.

MARKETING CRISIS

Every company faces marketing crises at intervals throughout its history. A company that fails to surmount one can slow to a halt, even atrophy, for many years. Just surviving such a test usually means only a return to the *status quo ante*.

But to triumph over such a crisis, to turn possible disaster into a resounding victory, can accelerate a company's growth in a burst of sustained business momentum. Meanwhile, such an unexpected turnabout can demoralize the competition or—at the very least—cause considerable discomfort.

Winning, beating the odds, converting defeat to victory—that's the point of marketing. The stories of such marketing coups are our business legends—what Iacocca did at Chrysler and what Townsend did at Avis. It is what Apple is trying to do right now in office automation.

And it is what Intel had to do in 1980. I know, because I was there. My career depended on a single victory.

Intel Corporation was founded in 1968 by Robert Noyce, the inventor of the integrated circuit, Gordon Moore, a legendary high-technology scientist and business strategist, and Andrew Grove, a now famous manager and executive.

Intel owed its success (Ben Rosen once called it the most important firm in America) to inventive genius, an ability to convert ideas into products (such as the famous microprocessor), Grove's dynamic management, and, not least, a talent for developing new markets for its new products. All those factors combined to give Intel one of the most remarkable starts in American business history.

But not all of Intel's success derived from intrinsic strengths. For a long time the company had also benefited from the benign neglect of more powerful firms in the same industry. Like many hot young electronics firms, Intel had focused on new markets, pursuing a path the industry giants had no interest in following. But the day of reckoning had come. By the mid-1970s Intel's achievements had become an embarrassment to its competitors and the target for most of the largest semiconductor manufacturers in the United States, Europe, and Japan. The list of competitors poised for attack was more than a little daunting: Texas Instruments, Motorola, National Semiconductor, Philips, Siemens, Nippon Electric Corporation (NEC), Hitachi, and Fujitsu, among others—the Billion Dollar Club of the semiconductor industry.

Intel still prospered but was losing ground in some important markets and was threatened in others. Intel once had been the leading supplier of 1,024-bit "dynamic" RAMs (random access memory) chips, but had lost that leadership to a start-up company. We had been unable to regain that momentum. A number of companies also had jumped into the EPROM (erasable programmable read only memory) chip market and were applying pressure. Finally, by 1979, Intel's strong position in the microprocessor market, though relatively intact, had suffered inroads from a start-up company named Zilog, and from Motorola, the latter a number of times Intel's size.

By late 1979 Intel was under full siege. Such attacks were nothing new to Intel, and the company had won more than its share of battles. But this threat was different in one very important way: The product line in dispute, the model 8086 16-bit microprocessor family, was the linchpin of the entire corporation. A number of multimillion-dollar Intel businesses depended on its success.

In particular, the sale of every Intel 8086 and its companion chip, the 8-bit 8088, pulled along large numbers of peripheral, memory, and controller chips worth in total ten times as much as the 8086. Whenever an 8086 sale was lost, the departing customer would frequently turn to the new supplier for those ancillary products. On top of that, Intel had two very profitable systems businesses dependent upon the success of the 8086.

Les Vadasz and I had been co-general managers of the microprocessor division in 1976 when the 8086 was being planned. At the time we decided to make the product an extension of the then-successful 8080 family. That created some design problems, but they were more than counterbalanced, in our opinion, by the resulting access to a large existing software library.

The 8086 was introduced to the market in 1978. As the first high-performance, fully supported 16-bit microprocessor, it had quickly gained the top position in the market, capturing the lead from older and less capable products supplied by Texas Instruments and National Semiconductoi. In response, Zilog and Motorola prematurely announced their own "paper tigers" (products that existed only on paper). Customers loved the features of the proposed products and were not too happy about some of the compromises Intel had made, so it was obvious that when and if those microprocessors ever emerged from the drawing boards, they would be a serious threat.

Meanwhile, as Intel had grown, the management had reorganized, and I left the microprocessor business to become the general manager of one of Intel's microprocessor-based systems businesses. Needless to say, any success I would have in my new role would be vitally dependent upon the survival of the 8086. So I remained in close touch with the 8086's marketing effort.

The 8086 marketing and sales group was suffering from apathy brought on by shattered morale. It was demoralizing to have one customer after the next lecture you about your employer's failures and your competitors' strengths. Many customers actually relished the opportunity to stick it to the famous Intel.

Some of the younger marketing people couldn't take the humiliation. It was easier to work on other projects. Being abused by customers—and even Intel's own sales force—wasn't fun.

Management encouragement had been ineffective at correcting what was becoming a destructive situation. In late November Don Buckout, an Intel field engineer on Long Island, sent management an incisive and desperate eight-page telex. The discussion of Buckout's telex at the executive staff meeting the following Tuesday couldn't have been more unpleasant. By the end of it I had either volunteered or been asked by Grove to run a marketing task force charged with solving the 8086 problem.

That was the beginning of Operation Crush.

ACTING FAST

A blue-ribbon group of the best sales and marketing people in the company was quickly assembled on December 4. We met continuously for three days. Among the "volunteers" were Jim Lally, the general manager of board products; Rich Bader, one of Jim's product managers; Dave House, the general manager of the microprocessor division; Jeff Katz, the marketing manager for microprocessors; Casey Powell, the regional manager to whom Buckout reported; and Regis McKenna, Silicon Valley's top marketing consultant. That was the first thing we did right. We did not delegate the job.

I appreciate that this runs counter to the principles in most textbooks on management and that many managers become trapped following such a path, but in the current crisis delegating responsibility had already failed. And, I would argue, the great marketing crusades of the past were led by the top people in the company: Lee Iacocca and Avis's Robert Townsend, to name two.

The first thing the group did was agree on the problem. That wasn't hard. There were three of us in the race: Motorola was going to be first, Zilog second, and Intel was headed for obscurity. All of us agreed that if we whipped Motorola, we would win. For that reason we made our goal not simply regaining market share but restoring Intel's preeminence in the market.

In the semiconductor business, the only market share you really care about is the one you maintain when the market is mature. To accomplish that, a firm must convince sufficient numbers of customers to "design in" (that is, integrate) your chip into their products. So the task force established a goal of achieving two thousand "design wins" by the end of 1980.

That was the second thing we did right. We had set a shockingly high goal. Knowledgeable observers thought a few hundred wins more reasonable. We decided that every salesman could get one win a month. By simple arithmetic, the number two thousand fell out. We trusted our people to come through.

As the discussion developed, we increasingly talked about what our real objective was. It was Jim Lally who articulated the need to "*crush* the competition." The word was wonderful. It captured the essence of our attitude. It also left no doubt about the single-mindedness of our purpose.

The code name Crush was never supposed to be made public. Roger Borovoy, the corporate counsel, was concerned about the implications of such a loaded word. But the name already was spreading like wildfire throughout the company. Everyone loved it. We had been kicked around enough; Crush signaled that we now meant to stand our ground and fight aggressively. And it meant we were going to win.

We decided to kick off the campaign before Christmas, not waiting until the first of the year. Now that we had a concept, there was no reason to defer action because of the holidays.

CRUSH INVENTS A PRODUCT

Our first task was to define the market and its competitive environment precisely. Hours were spend discussing customers and why we had won or lost various accounts. By the end of the discussion we had concluded that the customers could be divided into three general groups: hardware-oriented companies; software-oriented firms wanting to use Intel software; and software-oriented companies wanting to write their own software. We were doing well with the first two groups but nearly always lost out with the third.

That exercise all but confirmed what we already knew: Software-oriented customers, many of whom had migrated from the minicomputer field, wanted a microprocessor "architecture" (design) with precisely the features we lacked and Motorola and Zilog had. Moreover, those computer people did not really understand the ad-

5

vantages of the Intel products and were not crediting us with our strengths.

Thus, we decided, what we needed was a new product that better fitted the needs of our customer base. We would have to invent one.

Everyone on the task force accepted the harsh truth that Motorola and Zilog had better devices. If Intel tried to fight the battle only by claiming our microprocessor was better than theirs, we were going to lose. But we also knew that a microprocessor designer needed more than just the processor, and we had our competitors beaten hands down when it came to the extras. We had been playing to competitors' strengths, and it was time to start selling our own.

What were those strengths? We concluded that Intel's competitive advantages were these:

1. *A fine image as a technology leader:* Customers were concerned if they left Intel they would lose out on future developments.
2. *A more complete product family and a plan to enhance it:* Motorola was weak in this area. If we could make customers aware of that fact, it would be a great advantage to us.
3. *A well-focused and superbly trained technical sales force:* The Motorola sales force was a group of generalists. They lacked technical support in the field as well. Many were afraid of the microprocessor. We knew that if we could just get the customer to ask Intel before making a design decision, we usually could beat the competition.
4. *Better performance at the system level:* If the customer evaluated total capability—a system with the 8086, math co-processors and peripheral circuits—we came out ahead. We also had a well-thought-out interconnection scheme. Here, too, Motorola was weak.
5. *Ultimately, perhaps the most important advantage Intel had was that Motorola's customers were experiencing great difficulty making that chip work in their products.* Intel had great customer service and support. We could assure a customer's success with our device. By comparison, choosing the Motorola path clearly presented a risk to the customer.

By the end of the three-day meeting, we had a "product"—at the least the idea of one. We also had a preliminary schedule for delivering that product to market. Now, we needed to organize the company to deliver our message.

MOUNTING THE CRUSADE

The task force finished its preliminary work on a Friday. By the following Tuesday the multimillion-dollar program had been approved. Within a week the new strategy had been presented to the sales force and had earned its support.

I cannot stress the importance of that last step. Too often marketing programs are designed in an ivory tower. The sales force can instantly recognize a plan that will not work, so feedback from the field is critical. If the salespeople don't buy in at the outset, you should probably start over.

Fortunately, our sales force liked what it saw. The salespeople wanted a good fight as much as anyone in the firm, if not more.

Ultimately, Crush encompassed top management, the sales force, four marketing departments at three geographic locations, and a corporate communications group. All had to work together to pull off the internal portion of the operation. In all, Crush employed the talents of more than a thousand employees. The next big step would be to organize this army to march single-mindedly in one direction. The only common authority over the diverse organization was the president himself, Andy Grove.

Years later I learned that Dave Packard, one of the founders of Hewlett-Packard, used to say that marketing is too important to be left to the marketing department. If any event proved his point, it was the Crush kickoff meeting. It was held at the San Jose Hyatt House, with more than a hundred Intel managers in attendance.

As people walked in the door, they received a brown button with "Crush" spelled out in large orange letters (we used the orange color of the Denver Broncos, whose defensive team was referred to as the "Orange Crush" that year). The key speakers were Bob Noyce and Andy Grove. Bob let people know how important winning was to the company. Andy explained that Crush would remain a corporate focus until the job was done. As subtlety is not one of Andy's strengths, the managers had no doubt about what that statement meant.

There was a lot of work to be done. The key to accomplishing it all was getting everyone to do his or her share. The task force toured the company, explaining to groups the Crush plan and what we wanted the employees to do. Intel is a great place for teamwork, and people were quick to sign up.

The Crush crusade had begun.

The task force next chartered a number of interdepartmental committees to work out the details of implementation. That meant converting what until then had been mere ideas into actual plans of action. New sales aids were needed. System-level benchmarks had to be developed. Numerous articles had to be written for the trade magazines. An effort was even launched to get our customers to write about their experiences using the 8086. In all, more than fifty articles were published in the trade press.

We committed ourselves to preparing, within ninety days, a catalog of Intel's future products. That meant a massive effort writing preliminary data sheets on a large number of parts. In the end the new catalog ran more than a hundred information-packed pages. The "Futures Catalog," as it came to be called, served as a tangible demonstration of Intel's resurgent position in the market, a cornerstone for the seminar blitz that followed.

The seminar series was a tremendous enterprise. Our strategy was to focus first on large customers, as winning them was crucial. We had to make sure those customers appreciated the benefits of our products and our future plans in components, development systems, and software. For the first quarter we targeted twenty-five major customer seminars around the world. They were successful and were followed soon after by nearly fifty full-day seminars for the general public.

The seminars were attended by thousands of potential customers. One reason they came was to get a copy of the Futures Catalog. But to do that, each attendee had to register and fill out a qualification form. Intel then hired college students and put them in sales offices with the assignment to follow up on those leads. In most cases they were quite successful.

That burst of activity was merely a prelude to a climax: a users' forum at which we would discuss with our most important customers the in-depth details of our new products. To guarantee attendance at that event, we promised the top customers an opportunity to get together with Intel managers and engineers—not only to learn about our future plans but actually to influence them.

The seminar program turned out to be a tremendous drain on our corporate resources, but we didn't dare stop, because it was working. The morale in the field was picking up, the factory staff was feeling better, and most important, we had lured our principal competitor into fighting us on our own turf. Motorola even published its own "futures" catalog. As ours had been the result of dedicated efforts of entire marketing groups, Motorola's catalog seemed second-rate by comparison, adding to our credibility and undermining theirs.

Motorola's response to our announcement of a co-processor chip was a device that not only didn't solve the customers' problem but exposed the inadequacy of that firm's product line. Ultimately the Motorola catalog became an Intel sales tool, possibly the best one we had.

The one large client we had to win over was IBM. And we did—though why is still not clear to me. Dave House says IBM believed Intel had the only product that could be supplied in volume to support its needs. I myself suspect that availability of software for the Intel product line played the decisive role. The software existed in part because we had chosen to make the 8086 an extension of the 8080 and also because of the momentum built by Crush.

During all of this selling activity, Intel kicked off a big PR and advertising campaign. The old ad program was scrapped, and Regis McKenna created a new one around the theme, "There is only one high-performance VLSI computer solution—Intel delivers it." In support, Intel executives visited the business and trade press around the world.

At that point Operation Crush seemed to be working pretty well. The rate of design wins had picked up, as had the sale of development systems. We were monitoring our progress every two weeks, and by June things were looking good. In marketing, Dave House's groups delivered the sales support material on time, including the "Klingon Neutralization Kit," a 4-foot wooden box containing sales aids. "If the arguments did not work," he joked, "you could always drop it on the competition." We never had to; as far as we could tell, Motorola had already been stunned by the intensity of our effort.

Still, not everything had gone as planned. We appeared to be falling short of our goal of two thousand design wins.

When we kicked off Crush, we had promised the field salespeople a contest. Jim Lally was responsible for designing the program, and he had originally thought of sending the winners to Hawaii. As the program gained momentum, Tahiti was chosen as even more appealing. After all, these people were the key to the program, and they were killing themselves.

In June, as we looked at the numbers, it seemed we would fall far short of the goal. We became concerned that if there were only a very few winners, the contest would backfire. We would end up demotivating the sales force instead of motivating it. So we relaxed some of the criteria for validating a design win.

As it turned out, we didn't need to. The way Jim had designed the program, poor performance by a few could jeopardize the opportunity for others to win. By the third and fourth quarters, therefore, the peer pressure in the field on laggards was enormous. As important as all the other Crush activities were, the competition was probably the most important reason for our ultimate victory. The field was absolutely brutal in its pursuit of design wins and in self-enforcement.

In the end we did reach the two thousand design wins target. As a reward, almost the entire field sales force went on a trip to Paradise. They deserved it.

THE RESULTS

By the time Crush was over, our victory was almost complete. Intel all but owned the business application segment of the 16-bit microprocessor market. Today the Intel-type microprocessor architecture has about an 85 percent market share.

That result was far better than any of us would have dreamed possibie. Even if we had lost IBM, the company would have been better off because of Crush.

Still, we had failed to utterly Crush Motorola. Intel had beaten it in 8-bit and 16-bit microprocessors and had won the battle in the general-purpose microcontroller market, but that did not stop Motorola from entering the 32-bit battle. As I write, the two companies are again locked in a struggle for market share. Motorola is a much tougher company today. Its executives apparently learned as much from Crush as we did at Intel.

CRUSH IN HINDSIGHT

The process we at Intel went through with Operation Crush began as an intellectual exercise. We first had to understand the market segments and why were losing or winning in each of them. Once that was done, marketing could devise a product to meet the needs of the customer. We did not ask engineering to do anything different; that would have taken too much time. Time was the one thing we didn't have. So instead, we simply took the devices we had, adding Intel's credibility and a future direction, and then "dynamically repositioned" the product line (as Regis McKenna would say) as a complete solution. Marketing took what it had and created a "new" product line that the customers believed they needed. In the process we produced a strategy the field sales force could believe in.

Motorola also helped us. It had the opportunity to consolidate its victory yet instead fell into the trap of confronting our strengths head on. It could have been different but chose to be the same. Motorola had the chance to debunk our "futures" strategy as an act of desperation—which it was. Instead, our competitor legitimized our program by putting out an inferior imitation. Had Motorola chosen to remain aloof from our challenge, I think Intel would have been in deep trouble.

Motorola also had an incomplete product. It lacked many of the required peripherals and did not have the support to meet customer needs. Motorola couldn't assure its customers' success. Intel, on the other hand, could. Intel gave good service; Motorola (because it had failed to invest in the support infrastructure) could not. On top of that, Motorola had failed to realize it needed a different type of sales force to sell microprocessors. Intel had in place a group of specialists. We had been hiring people with computer backgrounds for a number of years, people who could effectively deal with the engineers who were our customers.

Probably the most important lesson that came out of Crush was a realization that a big crisis is best answered by a "crusade." Our greatest promotion was more an act of leadership than a flash of creative brilliance. Intel was loaded with product champions and marketing intellectuals, but in the final analysis what made Crush work was conviction and grit.

At Intel, people assumed that any problem could be solved. That made the job a lot easier. The team had no doubt that Regis McKenna would figure out how to position the product. It never entered Jim Lally's or Casey Powell's mind that we could fail. Their confidence was infectious.

Behind everything was Andy Grove, Intel's president, who supported the crusade with his time, energy, and conviction.

All the key ingredients—the organizations, the products, the people—had been there before Crush. The difference was that with Crush *we stopped cowering at the competition and started believing in ourselves.* As we regained our confidence, Intel exhibited hope rather than despair. The market sensed that change, and soon our customers were cheering on Intel's counterattack.

Yes, marketing is civilized warfare. In the pages that follow, I hope to teach you how to fight it.

TWO

The Winning Strategy

T HE DUTIES OF MARKETING are quite simple, yet few high-technology companies ever perform them. Why? Naïveté is one answer, but I suspect that in most cases the consequences of facing up to those responsibilities are so distasteful, companies refuse even to try.

For example, all companies should have the objective of being a leading supplier to their market. But few are willing to face their obligation to get out of a business if they don't achieve that goal. Instead, they wait to be driven out.

Other companies know they should target niches but hold to the hope of conquering the whole market with a "shotgun" approach. Still others would rather invent new products instead of performing the more arduous work on documentation, minor enhancements, and quality programs for existing ones. Only by such efforts will they find the great success they covet.

The fundamental truth of marketing comes down to this: If you are going to win the battle in the market place, you had better commit to the best strategy you can devise and implement it successfully. The market has no patience with sentiment. It rewards rational decisions executed with precision and conviction. Companies that succeed follow what might be called the "Strategic Principle" of marketing:

Marketing must invent complete products and drive them to commanding positions in defensible market segments.

If you are going to remember only one thing from this book, that principle and the reasons why it is true are it.

In the remainder of the chapter I shall elaborate on the strategic principle.

CRIMES IN THE NAME OF MARKET SHARE

In 1968 the Boston Consulting Group published its classic work on business strategies, *Perspectives on Experience.** It was the book that introduced most of us to the notion of experience curves and to the need to maximize market share. (There was more to it than that, but no one seemed to notice.) Since then it has become fashionable to engage in the mindless pursuit of market share. Companies are keenly aware of the importance of holding commanding positions in their markets. But in an attempt to achieve those positions, too many commit themselves to reckless pricing policies, ill-conceived strategic plans, and ineffective marketing programs. After years of pursuing market leadership, many of those companies have nothing to show for their efforts but red ink.

That is not to suggest the BCG experience curve theory is wrong. As a matter of fact, much of the recent success of Japanese industry has been based on its application. What is wrong is not the theory but a lack of understanding of its application and the market. Companies fight for market share in the wrong market place with the wrong product. Or else they engage in wars of attrition against competitors able to commit more resources to the battle over extended periods. Both are recipes for defeat.

It is time to look again at what the Boston Consulting Group really had to say.

The BCG argued, based on a great deal of empirical data it had accumulated from such diverse industries as semiconductors, petrochemicals, primary metals, and consumer products, that the total cost of doing business decreased 20 percent to 30 percent every time business experience (production) doubled. Thus, if business costs

Perspectives on Experience (Boston: The Boston Consulting Group, Inc., 1968).

follow a 30 percent experience curve, which they quite typically do in the semiconductor industry, the total cost of getting a particular product to the customer should fall 30 percent every time unit sales double. For example, when the accumulated volume of a one-dollar device increases from one million to two million units, the cost should fall to seventy cents.

The BCG concluded:

> In a rapidly growing product area, the most successful competitive strategy is to achieve and hold a dominant market position either through pricing (or equivalent) tactics or by segmenting the market into a sufficiently isolated segment which can be dominated. If it is concluded that market dominance cannot be achieved, then an orderly withdrawal from the business is probably the best plan.

Unfortunately, most businesses choose to focus on strategies to achieve incremental positions in broad markets. They are far less enamored with "segmenting the market into a sufficiently isolated segment which can be dominated." Many have paid dearly for that blunder.

About the same time as BCG finished its study, General Electric completed an extensive survey of businesses to determine what constituted the basic elements of success for both emerging and mature businesses. To the best of my knowledge, that document has remained confidential, but some of the conclusions did leak out. One of them was that companies with greater than a 30 percent market share were almost always profitable, and companies with less than 15 percent almost always lost money.

The clear inference one can draw from both studies is that a company must achieve a commanding position in a market place or die. Furthermore, the number of companies that can survive profitably in any market place is limited. Certainly no more than six companies can have greater than a 15 percent market share. In fact, a review of those two and other studies leads to the obvious inference that most markets end up with only two or three consistently profitable suppliers.

That's a disturbing conclusion. Still, one need only look around to see a number of profitable automotive suppliers, many computer companies, and numerous semiconductor manufacturers. How do they survive?

The answer is that markets are not as homogeneous as they first appear. There is not one automotive market, there are lots of them: small cars, big cars, medium-size cars, sports cars, inexpensive cars, luxury cars, imported cars, domestically manufactured cars, and on and on. Neither is there one wristwatch market. There are markets for disposable watches, watches worn as jewelry, fad watches, sport watches, mass-merchandised watches, and even scented watches. Similarly, for most classes of products there are numerous distinct market segments.

If those markets are distinct enough, then each can support two or three profitable suppliers. If they are large enough, a number of others can struggle along in them as well.

The point is that a company does not have to be as big as IBM to make a profit in the computer business, or as big as GM to make money in automobiles; *it only has to be large in its own protected market segment.* The market segment it serves may be isolated from competition by barriers to ward off competitive attacks, or it may survive because of the benign attitude of competition.

The problem most companies have in coming to grips with market share is in understanding market segmentation. The crimes committed in the name of market share are not a result of going for market share in and of itself. They result from pursuing market share in a haphazard fashion—usually in too broad a market.

The goal should never be only to capture a very small percentage of a huge market. Rather, concepts must be developed and resources identified to gain significantly greater than a 15 percent market share in a *well-protected* market segment. Anything else is to plan for failure.

DIVIDE AND CONQUER

Technology companies, when faced with massive competition, inevitably come up with the same tactic: to attack market segments, vertical markets, and niches. But, having proclaimed that strategy, they usually proceed as if the statement alone were all that is needed to succeed.

Market segmentation is one of the most discussed and least understood concepts in business. For that reason it is worthwhile relating to you one of my experiences in segmenting a market.

When I arrived at Intel in 1973, it was obvious that soon a number of potentially large businesses would be established based on the marketing of low-cost microcomputer systems. There already were several companies building hobby kits using microprocessors and selling them in reasonable volume.

I had my own vision of what the microcomputer market was going to be like. I imagined huge numbers of customers walking through the front door demanding to buy thousands of microprocessor chips.

The reality was significantly different. I was amazed by the number of customers trying to use micros in low-volume—many less than fifty chips a year—applications. The customers were having problems. Some couldn't make the hardware work, and others did not know how to write the software. This group of customers had a unique collection of needs. They represented a market segment.

What was even more interesting was that I found most of our potential competitors had the same skewed image of the market as I had entertained. They too thought most customers were buying micros by the thousands. (They probably had been reading Intel ads.)

So here was a big market segment walking in the door, begging for help, and being ignored by the industry.

As Bob Garrow (a top-notch systems engineer), Jim Lally, and I talked about that unrecognized market, we became more and more convinced it offered a terrific opportunity. We theorized about the ideal product for those people: the single-board computer. Our competitors had toyed with similar ideas, but none had really developed the type of system we were convinced the market needed. After all, we reasoned, microprocessors were only going to get cheaper. It was inevitable then that systems of the future would be crammed with them. If we could come up with a product that would make it easy for customers to use multiple processors in their systems, we would have a competitive edge.

There were, of course, some serious problems with the market. Digital Equipment Corporation was one of them. It was the world's leading minicomputer manufacturer and was working its way down into "our" product area. Although DEC did not yet have a true single-board computer, it had a competitive alternative.

Fortunately, DEC was not paying much attention to this new business; it was occupied with building bigger and better minicomputers.

Another problem with the market was its apparent low cost of entry. Engineering the types of devices we planned required little development effort. That meant, if we were successful, other firms would soon chase us.

To blunt the prospective attacks, we did several things. One move was to develop a new interface or "bus" structure to enable our customers to link multiple microprocessors into a single system.

"Multibus," as it was called, became an industry standard, and we freely licensed it to all would-be competitors. That was in direct opposition to DEC's strategy of "protecting" its bus structure from use by competitors. It helped to differentiate Intel from DEC, but it created myriad small competitors. However, we were confident we could deal with them. DEC was the real problem. As a result of licensing, Intel enjoyed a large number of add-on suppliers who expanded and enriched the product line and created some new niche markets. Further, our product was specifically targeted to the needs of Intel's existing customer base. Therefore, our sales and distribution channels were perfect for the job. DEC (and other competitors) did not have as good contact with the electrical engineering community, and that gave Intel a further advantage. Thus, when a microprocessor customer contacted Intel, and lots did, our salesperson could first find out if the prospect was a potential system customer and, if so, could attempt to sell a single-board computer.

Those were not our only advantages. Since Intel was designing components on one side of the house and systems on the other, we were able to make use of some of our newest chips long before they were available to the market—and to our competitors. Add to this Intel's brand image in the microprocessor market, and we had lots of big advantages. As the market developed, we differentiated ourselves even further by adding software, more proprietary products, and specialized distribution channels.

All of those things created barriers to market entry. As a result, the single-board computer business became large and profitable for Intel. The business, started with a $500,000 investment, long ago passed $100 million in revenues and enjoyed profit margins above the corporate average. Multibus's market share passed DEC's, and Intel is far and away the leading supplier of multibus products. Semiconductor companies, such as NEC, National, and Advanced Micro Devices (AMD), who raced Intel for the market, have dropped out. Intel now stands almost alone in this maturing market segment, protected by barriers difficult to cross.

That is what market segmentation is all about.

WHAT IS A MARKET SEGMENT?

Like many concepts in marketing, the notion of a "market segment" is deceptively simple. A market segment is a group of customers sharing common desires, needs, and buying patterns. But in actual practice a marketing department that talks to enough customers will gather sufficient data to define enough market segments to guarantee confusion and paralyze any management team.

The real challenge in making market segmentation work is to identify the dominant characteristics in a customer population, then to create a product satisfying the needs arising from those characteristics. Much of the brilliant work done in consumer marketing and retailing results from keen insight, sometimes developed through painstaking research, as to what new products will have great appeal to a select customer group. Think of the Ford Mustang, the Swatch, and Miller Lite Beer.

Market segments are not neat and tidy. A single consumer can easily belong to many. Segments are the nonexclusive country clubs of marketing. The same consumer may enjoy shopping in both Neiman-Marcus and K-mart. Such bimodal behavior means that he or she won't fit neatly into any simplistic market analysis. Consumer migration from one segment to another can depend on things as simple as the length of time since the last paycheck.

WHAT CREATES MARKET SEGMENTS?

The forces segmenting markets are numerous. No single book could or should list all of them. What is important is understanding the types of customer preferences that go into creating segments.

Markets are most obviously segmented by product characteristics. High-tech companies tend to concentrate on that aspect. One group of customers may want to purchase only low-cost, "dumb" terminals; another, for reasons of productivity, may want high-performance, "intelligent" ones. Some customers for graphics work stations are happy with inexpensive low-power models, but Lucasfilms wants the ultimate graphics work station on which to fight the next *Star Wars*.

Capacity requirements are also important in segmenting markets. Customers needing large quantities of a product, such as General Motors, will do business with companies that have a high volume capability or have the financial resources to build it. The supplier unable to meet volume needs undermines that customer's business and quickly earns a reputation as a "boutique" manufacturer. The customer feelings that can develop as a result of supplier-caused shortages are very difficult to overcome.

In Japan, where much of the manufacturing is volume-oriented, suppliers tend to link up with a few very large customers. Their commitment is to the most-favored customers, often to the exclusion of all others. The less-favored customer in Japan is thus quite vulnerable. Unable to trust its source of supply, it seeks out other manufacturers. In that way buyer–seller relationships and customer wariness about those relationships create market segments in Japan (and, increasingly, here).

Quality, distribution channels, brand image, services, price, geography, level of documentation, customer comfort with corporate policy, customer needs for credit, the ability of users to relate to a supplier's management, and the flexibility of suppliers, their ability to alter capacity to meet customers' requirements, are some of the other factors segmenting markets.

The high-tech market for any device is not homogeneous. It is in fact tens of markets, many differing dramatically from the others. The individual market segments are varied and forever shifting. A product feature is meaningless one day and the next day all-important. Every difference in features and each shift in customer preference creates an opportunity for exploitation by an alert marketing team to gain a competitive advantage in a market segment.

HEAD ON IS HEADSTRONG

To access a market segment requires an investment as unique as the segment itself. That investment may be small, such as changing the color of a product. Or it may be quite large. A product line may have to be redesigned to meet new performance requirements. A new channel of distribution may have to be found.

The level of investment required of an outsider to enter a new market creates a *segment* or *entry* barrier. The segment barriers between two competitors will differ depending on their market position. If two companies serve similar segments, it may be relatively inexpensive for one to cross over into the other's market. For example, if two companies share many of the same distributors, as they do in the semiconductor business, the cost of attacking a competitor's market is significantly reduced.

Segment barriers become very large as an industry matures. If companies would only take the time to analyze the most important segment barriers facing them before they assault a competitor, a lot of misery could be avoided. *Too much attention in business plans is focused on what a company plans to do, not on whether those plans are adequate relative to the complete set of segment barriers the company will face.*

Think of the barrier created by a big sales force. A digital system company sells approximately $1 million of products per salesperson per year. Achieving $1 billion in sales requires a sales force of a thousand salesmen, each costing the company about $100,000 a year. Therefore, at a billion-dollar sales level, the company is spending approximately $100 million a year on field sales. A small company with only ten salesmen and $10 million in revenues simply cannot compete with that. It must attack a niche.

The barriers to entry into soft drink markets can be very formidable as well. The advertising dollars required to build a nationwide brand image for a cola product are measured in the hundreds of millions of dollars. But even if one spends the money, the problems have just begun. A new competitor soon finds the biggest distributors in a given city already carry either Coca-Cola or Pepsi and aren't interested in bottling another brand.

Everywhere one looks, the companies that are profitable in their markets are protected by significant barriers. Find a good business, and you will undoubtedly find substantial barriers. For example, Tandem Computer supplies large, nonstop transaction processing computers. Its products are protected by massive hardware and software investments, in-depth application expertise, and a customer base whose confidence in Tandem is difficult to shake.

Segment barriers become strategically important when the cumulative cost of crossing them is large compared to the value of the market. When the cost of entering and gaining a position in a market becomes as high as the potential profits, then competitors are effectively barred. On the other hand, if the cost of crossing the barriers is only a small percentage of total market size, many will attempt to cross. A few will no doubt succeed. That situation exists most frequently when there is no dominant supplier to the market.

But even if the barriers are large, if the market is sufficiently attractive some companies will not be deterred. Technology companies are notoriously reckless when it comes to market entry. They tend to concentrate on the cost of developing and manufacturing a product rather than on the cost of crossing segment barriers. Thus many enter into a market chase naïvely.

What is the true cost of entering a market? I have a rule of thumb.

(To see how I developed it, see Appendix A.) The cost of entering a market against a well-managed competitor with an undifferentiated product—if such a thing can really exist—is 70 percent of the sales of the leader. From this it follows that the cost of crossing the segment barriers required to enter a market is:

$$.7 \times (\text{leader's share of market}) \times (\text{the size of the market})$$

The formula explains why it is so difficult to enter the market when there is an entrenched leader. It also explains why companies such as Intel, Control Data Corp. (CDC), and DEC were able to enter large markets with very few resources. Simply put, they got there first, before an established competitor existed. Head-on assaults against entrenched competitors are usually suicidal. Conversely, once a company achieves a commanding position, competitors must make large investments if they hope to dislodge it with a head-on attack.

SEGMENTATION LETS DAVIDS SLAY GOLIATHS

Targeting a market segment makes participation less costly for a company and attack significantly less attractive for a competitor. To be a supplier to a broad market usually demands a broad product line. On the other hand, focusing on a segment means a leaner, tighter product family. That means reduced R&D costs.

Segmented markets also can be attacked with specialized distribution channels: A sales force of specialists can operate at significantly higher efficiency than the huge sales force of a broad-line competitor. Specialized distributors often have excellent market knowledge and contacts, which can be exploited. There may be a number of vertical trade shows and publications serving the customer base, which can be used economically to promote a product. Vertical promotions are far more cost-effective than horizontal ones.

Focus has other salutary effects. When a company commits to a narrow market, its best people can devote their attention to learning one segment, building their corporate image in the segment, and developing products to serve that precise customer base. Also, when the resources of a company are devoted to a specific market, the cumulative investment can become quite large compared to other competitors and to the market itself. For example, all advertising dollars can be devoted to building brand acceptance in the segment. Specialized products and options can be developed to satisfy the unique needs of the customer base.

With all those advantages, a small company frequently can gain such a large share of a market segment that it makes no economic sense for a competitor to pursue the business.

By segmenting a market a small company can match the resources of a much larger competitor and at the same time build a defensible position. Segmentation makes it possible for companies with limited resources to build commanding positions.

IN HIGH-TECH YOU ARE NEVER SAFE

Now, after trumpeting the value of market segments, it's time for the bad news. There are several effective strategies to break down entry barriers. In a rapidly changing business you must always be on the lookout for a competitive attack. If you become complacent because of a big lead, someone will discover a good way to take your business away from you. The attacks will usually come from followers or from a market entrant using a new technology.

In commodity markets, playing the follower often works well. The Japanese have long used this strategy successfully. The GE study explains why. It identified two successful business strategies, one for leaders and the other for followers. The leadership strategy requires large investments both in R&D to develop new products and in marketing to develop the new market. Those costs seldom go away but live on, burdening product lines with high costs.

The follower does just the opposite. This firm copies a competitor or obtains a technology license. It spends little money on market development. Because the follower builds up its capacity after the leader, it can frequently take advantage of newer and more efficient manufacturing techniques. That's what the Japanese did in the steel industry.

The follower strategy in a commodity market gives a company low overhead, low manufacturing costs, and price leadership. Buyers are attracted by the opportunity to get a high-quality product in volume, on time, and at a bargain price. The strategy usually works well because market leaders allow it to. They are slow to react to the evolution of their market from specialty goods to commodities.

In other cases a single attack based on a new technology can destroy a leading supplier and reshuffle competition.

The semiconductor business provides many excellent examples of that effect. In the 1960s most computers used magnetic cores for their main memories. The suppliers to the market set up low-cost manufacturing facilities in Asia to string the tiny cores manually into arrays. Those firms constantly reduced the cost and improved the performance of their product.

But by the early 1970s, when Intel ran an ad with a headline, "The End: Cores Lose Price War to New Chip," it really was "the end" for most core suppliers. Semiconductor technology provided customers with faster and ultimately lower-cost memory technology. The core manufacturers' investments in design and manufacturing counted for nothing.

In slower-moving fields, the displacement of one competitor by another can take years. But in high-tech fortunes can change overnight. Companies at the forefront of technology truly balance on the razor's edge.

Over the years I have both won with technological breakthroughs and been the victim of them. I remember most vividly the defeats. I watched Intel's market share slip away in the development system business because of a change in technology. Many customers decided they wanted to do their work on large "super minicomputers" instead of on our microprocessor-based systems. Try as we might to deal with the problem, the effects of the shift were devastating. I watched dedicated followers, principally the Japanese, take market share from us in the mature components businesses. They executed their strategy well, and we had no effective response.

A company can lose a big lead if it fails to adjust its cost structure as its products evolve from specialty items to commodities or if it fails to exploit new technologies. Commanding positions do not ensure a permanent place in the market. The minute you think you are safe in a high-tech market segment, you have sown the seeds of your own defeat.

MYTHS ABOUT MARKET ENTRY

Companies are often deceived by markets that offer easy entry then turn out to be murderous to stay in. Often the cost of developing a device to sell in a market is confused with that of establishing a leading position in that market. Companies forget that even with a good device they still haven't entered a market until they have established a significant position. Just as frequently, if a device is difficult to develop, management thinks the market must be difficult to enter.

Everyone knows how easy entry was into the PC business. For a few million dollars or less, a company could develop enough of a product to join the race. The truth is, massive markets require massive investments of resources. A small company such as Apple could successfully enter the market when the market was small and the barriers low. By getting in early, Apple was able to amass the necessary resources to have a large impact. The companies that followed could not. The market by then was more mature. In order to develop and sustain a position, the latecomers would have had to make investments equal to a significant proportion of the leader's annual sales. Few had such resources.

What it comes down to it this: There are very few markets where it is easy to achieve a commanding position after day one. Market entry is usually very difficult for late entrants.

GO FOR SEGMENT MARKET SHARE

In recent years a number of well-known companies, large and small, have vanished. That phenomenon has been most visible among high-tech start-up companies with initial success in the market place. Some made a little money, went public, then died.

There are thousands of reasons why companies go out of business, but a frequent one is a failure by a company to achieve a commanding position in a well-defended market segment. The shakeout phenomenon, which outsiders observe with morbid fascination, is the manifestation of this problem. Today it is the PC companies, yesterday it was the electronic calculator manufacturers, tomorrow it will be the computer-aided engineering vendors. *The companies that will vanish will be those that didn't make themselves unique in their customers' minds.*

Remarkably, many of the victims never even "planned" to succeed. They never appreciated the resources required to establish a leading position and maintain it. Frequently they attempted to retreat to a smaller market segment only after they had lost the bigger war.

And usually the retreat was accompanied by large writeoffs and debilitating layoffs. By then they were already doomed.

Many companies enter businesses planning to capture only a small percentage of the market. Such plans are not conservative; they are extremely dangerous. They are strategies for failure. The only good plans and the only good marketing programs are those aimed at dominance, backed by sufficient resources to achieve it, and executed with precision.

ENGINEERS INVENT DEVICES

The "miraculous" Intel electronic watch was a flop. The "wonderful" TI personal computer, even when pitched by the redoubtable Bill Cosby, failed. The problems were the same. The technologists created a good device, but marketing failed to invent a good product. Both firms tried to market something that satisfied only a portion of customers' needs. They built only partial products.

A true product is a very complex thing; it has a multitude of dimensions, all changing and evolving. Its features can be eroded by competition or transformed to pursue a shifting customer base.

Great devices are invented in the laboratory. Great products are invented in the marketing department.

Consider the invention of the microcomputer. In 1969 Busicom, a Japanese calculator company, visited Intel to discuss its idea for custom large-scale integrated (LSI) circuits to be used in a new calculator. Busicom wanted Intel to design twelve different circuits. Ted Hoff was heading Intel's applications effort at the time. Ted quickly realized there was no practical way to implement the devices proposed by the Japanese.

A computer man at heart, Ted was sure a small general-purpose computer could do the job. Further, he believed that everything could be fabricated from just three types of integrated circuits. That was the birth of the microprocessor.

I ran into Bob Noyce and Ted Hoff in the fall of 1969 at a computer conference in Las Vegas. We discussed future trends in integrated circuits. I described my concept for a "bipolar"-type circuit set that could do for high-speed applications what Ted's invention had done for less speed-intensive ones. A year later I joined a company that tried unsuccessfully to implement my idea. We had a good system design, but we lacked the requisite semiconductor technology.

In late 1971 I watched with envy as Intel announced the first microprocessor to the world. I now understood why Bob and Ted had been so interested in our Las Vegas conversation. Nevertheless, the stillborn product I was working on had some important implications for Intel, and I brought some of those ideas with me when I joined the firm in 1973. The key one was the concept of device emulation. That idea and many others were useful in augmenting Intel's product offering.

When I joined Intel I was stunned to learn how small the microprocessor business really was. In fact, Intel was selling less than $1 million a month of microprocessors, memories, and simulator boards. The market was slow to develop because of limitations in the devices and because most customers, frankly, didn't know what to do with them and couldn't get them to work in systems.

By 1974 a lot of new microprocessors were arriving in the market. Rockwell had the PPS-8; Motorola was ready to announce the 6800. Other companies had products in the wings. Intel's new device, the 8080, also made its debut that year.

In a comparatively short time the 8080 became the hands-down winner in the microprocessor market. The reason it won was not only that Ted Hoff and his technical team invented a superb *device* but because Intel invented the first broad market microprocessor *product*. One of the factors in turning the 8080 into a complete product was a device emulator based on concepts developed in my prior job.

The Intel 8080 was the most complete microcomputer product in its day. It was much more than the "chip." It comprised the "chip," to be sure, but also application notes, ads, microprocessor development systems and emulators, software, field applications engineering and single-board computers, customer education programs, and Bob Noyce's ability to capture the public imagination.

There were many inventors of the microprocessor. Certainly Ted Hoff and his crack technical team invented Intel's microprocessor families, but those were just devices. There were hundreds of other creative people who made contributions to the invention of the product. Intel had those people, and that is why it won the early microprocessor battles against other companies that entered the market with only devices.

In truth, thousands of devices are invented every year. Some, like my bipolar microprocessor, never see the light of day because of technical problems. Others emerge as only partial products, already as doomed in the market place as if they had never made it off the engineers' desks.

That is not to denigrate the role of the engineer-inventor. All the marketing hype in the world can't create a product unless a device exists. But the key is to convert great devices into great products.

Everyone knows what a product is. It is what you buy at the store, the services of a doctor, or the advice of a consultant. Interestingly, the device often obscures the product. When shopping for food, the food (the device) is being purchased, but so are the retail environment, the display of the food, the cleanliness of the store, and the ease of parking (the product). People at a Rolling Stones rock concert are there to hear the group but also are buying a place in a social environment and the chance to brag to their associates afterward. A product is the totality of what a customer buys. It is the physical device or service from which the customer gets direct utility plus a number of other factors, services, or perceptions, which make the product useful, desirable, and convenient. When a *device* is properly augmented so that it can be easily sold and used by a customer it becomes *product*.

Incomplete or partial products are the misfits and deviates of the market place. They are the source of a great many high-tech marketing failures. (Henceforth we shall retain this semantic distinction between "devices" and "products.")

CREATING COMPLETE PRODUCTS IS EXPENSIVE

Complexity is the hallmark of high-tech products. They are more complicated than most consumer products. The complete product called a "computer," for example, consists of system hardware and a wide array of associated options, an operating system, application languages, application programs, documentation, customer training, salesman and presale application support, postsale application support, the maintenance organization and the logistic system that supports it with spare parts, the brand image of the company, the advertising and public relations about the system, and most importantly the feeling of confidence the customer has in the supplier. A company with only a few of those characteristics faces a problem similar to trying to sell an unpainted car. A customer will purchase it, but only at a very cut rate.

That complexity is perhaps the most fascinating aspect of high-technology products. The computer industry, still rapidly evolving, has provided a series of examples of the agony of partial products. Such large companies as GE, RCA, and Xerox tried building computer products but lacked an appreciation of what a complete product was. They failed in part because they underestimated what it would take to complete their computer system offering. For some applications their computers lacked software, for others they did not have the right kinds of peripherals. In many cases they were deficient in their ability to deliver high-quality product service. In almost all cases they lacked sufficiently broad sales coverage to create needs and solve problems for the customer.

GE struggled for years with unending losses. System after system was introduced, each claiming to be better than competitors' products. In spite of all efforts, customers did not buy GE computers in sufficient numbers. No matter what the company did, it always seemed to lack a product feature or service required by the customer.

In an attempt to broaden its product line, strengthen its peripheral product offering, and increase the capacity of its overseas distribution channels, GE purchased a French computer manufacturer and a portion of Olivetti. GE also narrowed its market focus (retreated to niches) with the hope of offering more complete solutions. It didn't work.

Finally, in the late 1960s, a frustrated GE appointed a strategic task force to study why the firm had not gained sufficient market share to be a viable competitor in the mainframe computer business. Reportedly the group concluded that each percentage point of market share gained would require an investment of more than $100 million. In the computer business the cost of completing a product is very large indeed. It is very high in most other businesses as well. *The cost of creating a complete product is often many times the cost of developing the device.*

DEFINING A HIGH-TECHNOLOGY PRODUCT

It's difficult to describe what a true high-technology product is. The very existence of most high-tech companies is predicated on developing new products and exploiting new businesses. Thus there are no well-worn paths to follow. One may not be able to find a prior group that did things almost right and left behind a business plan to be improved upon. It's also difficult to find failure models in a new field. They usually occur at the same time a leader is succeeding, often because of that success. It is thus almost impossible to study the mistakes made and the strategies and tactics that did not work. Role models are scarce.

One exciting new software business area is the "silicon compiler." These programs simplify and speed the design of integrated circuits. Few of these "devices" have been developed, and none are yet "products." To date, six silicon compiler companies have been founded, with more to follow. Each has a different strategy. Their proposed products are likewise different. It is anyone's guess what finally will be required to make a silicon compiler a complete product. Market research will be of little help, because potential customers won't know many of the subtle things they want until they get the product.

One of the leaders in the silicon compiler field is VLSI Technology, Inc. (VTI). It claims to offer its customers a complete cradle-to-grave service. The sales pitch is great, but the product is in no way complete. For some customers the human interface is too complex. Others want more extensive circuit libraries. For a few the software will not support their highly complex designs. Documentation and training are inadequate for another large portion of potential customers. Finally, the company's design centers are not convenient for many.

Is VTI doing a bad job? No. In fact, it is a leader in the field. But tens of millions of dollars more will have to be spent to complete the product. For VTI the most important objective is to achieve for its products a higher degree of completeness than that of any of its competitors' products. To do so VTI will have to segment the market. That won't be easy: It will not be obvious which segments are largest. Nor can the company be sure whether a target market can be developed if key parts of the finished product are still missing. Early users of any new and highly complex technology product almost always find some essential features missing. Will they stick around and wait for those additions to be completed?

A frequently made high-tech marketing mistake is to underestimate the number of dimensions a product must have. New devices are constantly being introduced to the market, yet technology companies continue to put their faith in good devices alone. They continue to ignore the importance of the complete product.

Most high-tech companies would be horrified to sell a device that did not work, but a large percentage seem able to tolerate devices that cannot be used because of inadequate training or inaccurate documentation. The ultimate problem for the customer is the same: If the device can't be made to work, for whatever reason, it is useless. Similarly, high-tech companies are more concerned over the manufacturability of products than whether the distribution channels can sell them. Products bought by a distributor are not automatically sold to the customer. That lesson cost TI more than $100 million in the home computer business. Devices that don't work or can't be manufactured are incomplete products, but so are products that can't be successfully applied or sold.

A great deal of technical creativity goes into developing new devices. Far too little energy is expended on inventing complete products. The latter requires marketing innovation.

AN EVOLVING CUSTOMER BASE
CHANGES THE PRODUCT

Customer needs and desires define products. As they change, so must the product. Evolving customers demand evolving products. During the life cycle of a product its customer base may change radically.

There is a well-known customer evolution: Innovators buy the first offering of a new high-technology product, then early adaptors and followers, and finally the late adaptors. The precise definition of those customer types is not important. What is important is that the device must be packaged as a different product for each group.

The "innovator" wants to be the first to use a new device. He will usually tell the salesperson his company is a technological leader and must stay ahead. He can't afford to wait; he even wants to be a test site. He delights in telling his suppliers' engineers just what is wrong with the new device or service. He wants to be part of the creation of the new product. For him a complete product is frequently a sadly incomplete one. He expects it to have poor documentation and many bugs. He is also willing to take the chance that the device may be delinquent and delay his own schedule.

On the other extreme, late adaptors, for psychological or sound business reasons, are not driven to use the latest innovations. Many are associated with businesses where the cost of mistakes is large and little is to be gained from risk-taking. Late adaptors are interested in complete and proven products and are frustrated by product malfunctions or errors in documentation. A good example of a late adaptor is an automobile company, which *must* use proven products in high

30

volume. To do otherwise would risk painful recalls and production line shutdowns.

The story of the personal computer business exemplifies how a market evolves. The innovators who purchased the first Altairs and Apples were mainly computer freaks who liked to play with the system and make it perform interesting tricks by programming it in arcane "machine language." Some early users were even sharp enough to modify hardware.

The real growth in the market came when application software became available for personal computers. The spreadsheet program Visicalc is sometimes described as the computer program that made Apple successful. That overstates the case, but Visicalc did enable Apple to sell many of its systems for business applications. Considerable amounts of application software written by independent software vendors (ISVs) turned the early Apples into complete products for the education market. Independent programmers wrote books about how to use the Apple, making up for the poor documentation that came with the product. Those contributions helped "complete" the Apple for certain market segments. Eventually the product evolved to the point where it was useful not only to innovators but to early adaptors, some followers, and a few late adaptors.

The personal computer sold today is a dramatically different product from the one Apple originally introduced. Interestingly, though the Apple became a much more mature product than when it was introduced and was used in a great many business applications, it was still vulnerable to a more complete product, the IBM PC. The PC was able to displace the Apple because of some important product features, excellent brand image, and strong distribution. The IBM label legitimized the PC for professional business applications. The PC became the complete product for business applications and turned the Apple into a device for that market.

Most high-tech products mature rapidly and in an agonizing fashion. A frequent mistake is to underestimate the degree of completeness required by the market. Often a company enters a market late with a device when measured against the existing market standards. The device might be a product for a market made up of innovators, but it will be inappropriate for the followers. So the product flops. Companies focus too much on the device, assuming that if it can just be made better success will inevitably follow. The truth is, *too much time is spent comparing one device to another and not enough comparing products.*

A product will achieve a commanding position within a market segment only if it is complete. Failure to complete a product leaves it vulnerable to attacks by competition. Marketing is the organization within a business charged with the responsibility for ensuring products are complete. It is also marketing's job to guarantee that the product remains complete over time as the customer base evolves and the competition sets new standards for completeness. That means regular reviews of every dimension of a product.

MARKETING INVENTS PRODUCTS

The Inventors' Hall of Fame contains the names of many creative geniuses. Surprisingly, few of those people ever invented a product. They certainly conceived of technological breakthroughs, and they are all great people. But all invented *devices.*

The Inventors' Hall of Fame does not recognize many creators of great *products.* Missing are Lee Iacocca, the inventor of the Ford Mustang and the New Chrysler Corporation, and Ray Kroc, who created McDonald's.

Those marketing triumphs were a result of creative thinking and hard work. They are the products of *marketing invention.* Once the device is sound, good marketing adds the rest. Promotional programs are developed to inform the customer about the product and to create interest. Services, such as application engineering and training, are added to ensure that the customer will achieve satisfactory use. New applications are discovered for the device, frequently not the ones envisioned by those who developed it. This demands as much inventiveness as the original experiments in the laboratory. Companies make big mistakes when they confuse device and product invention. Devices won't succeed over the long term in the market. That's why marketing invention is essential. It turns devices into products.

WHY HIGH-TECH MARKETING
IS DIFFERENT

Marketing is characterized by diversity. Even marketing departments of companies in the same business may differ dramatically. Marketing functions in companies in different businesses will vary even more.

For example, in some industries salespeople call on customers. In others they call on retailers. Distributors in the electronic components industry sell products directly to the consumers, while in many other industries distributors sell products only to retailers. In high-tech, products are usually sold to the customer by salespersons. In consumer products they are sold principally by advertising, packaging, and tasteful display.

Technology marketing differs from other types of marketing because of its emphasis on functions nonexistent or unimportant in other fields. In the computer business and related fields it is common to find companies spending more than 20 percent of revenues on direct sales, service, and postsale support. In most technology companies a tremendous amount of money is also spent on product documentation. By comparison, advertising and promotional expense amount to only a few percentage points of sales. In technology companies most of the marketing effort is devoted to direct sales, training and supporting distribution channels, customer education and application support, service, and postsale support.

In consumer businesses marketing budgets are allocated differently. Marketing puts considerable effort into designing packages and into advertising and promoting the product. Promotional budgets frequently run more than 10 percent of sales. Consumer marketing groups are expert at creating customer "pull." The customer is sold the product by promotions designed to create end demand. The salesperson calls on retail outlets and fights for shelf space, almost never dealing with the customer. Consumer product companies don't spend a great deal of their resources on postsale support, documentation, and customer education. Instructions aren't needed with tubes of toothpaste or cigarette packs. The documentation costs for a bottle of aspirin are quite small.

The decision to purchase a consumer product is usually a low-risk one, as most are relatively inexpensive. If a customer is not happy with a purchase, it can be returned or thrown away. For inexpensive products, consumer awareness is key to sales. A good advertising campaign can motivate customers to seek out a product and buy it.

In contrast, technology products are almost never sold by advertising. At best, advertising only raises customer awareness and creates a desire to learn more about the product. That's because the purchase of a high-tech product is often a high-risk decision. When a customer is going to spend thousands and sometimes hundreds of thousands of dollars, impulse buying is rare.

Often the truth about a high-technology product is not known until months after it is purchased. Some pieces of capital equipment can't really be evaluated for years. That is true of much of the equipment used to build advanced semiconductors, as well as of computer systems. A company making a large data processing installation may spend much of a decade getting it to work properly.

When customers make decisions like those, the intangible factors become important. Customers evaluate suppliers on how well they will perform and on how much they can be trusted. Customers ask of a potential supplier: Will you really fix the software bugs? Will you really be available to service my equipment in two hours? Will you really be in business five years from now? Will you really complete work on the software modification on time?

The market for many new high-tech products is becoming increasingly consumer-like. That has prompted many high-tech companies to employ numbers of consumer marketing types. They have frequently failed when they have strictly applied consumer marketing techniques. The reason is that the application of those techniques is insufficient to complete the product. Technology products can benefit greatly from consumer techniques, but by themselves they are not enough.

Advertising helps to create trust but is only a small part of the selling process. Reputation, service, support, and references are more important. Those and many other factors make marketing high-tech different.

PRODUCT COSTS ARE DOMINATED BY MARKETING

In more and more technology businesses, the price of the product is dominated by the cost of marketing. In personal computers the cost of distributing a product is frequently greater than 40 percent of the sale price. Computer retailers receive 65 percent gross margins on product options. The advertising and marketing expense can run another 10 percent. Meanwhile the cost of actually manufacturing the product is often less than 25 percent of the recommended sale price. Thus distribution and marketing costs can be more than twice the manufacturing cost. In the mainframe computer business the costs of selling, supporting, and educating the customer are approximately equal to the cost of making the equipment. For the early microprocessor, customers were so thirsty for information that the cost of providing them with "free" manuals actually exceeded the cost of making the product. Software products cost almost nothing to make.

During its life cycle, the cost of completing a product can change dramatically. For example, some products become commodities in a relatively short time. For them the cost of marketing usually falls. Other products, sold to an increasingly broad application base, may require more and more support. There, the cost of marketing will increase as the product matures.

For the near future at least, the costs of manufacturing increasingly complex devices, driven principally by advances in microelectronics and automation, are going down, while the costs of distribution and service are heading up. The customer, of course, is concerned only with the cost of the product, not with whether the price is driven by manufacturing or marketing costs. The firms that succeed will be those paying attention to getting complete products to the customer in a more cost-effective fashion. For many products, squeezing the last penny out of manufacturing may not be as important as ensuring efficient operation of the sales and marketing functions. Many products won't be able to achieve commanding positions in the market unless they are marketed in a cost-effective fashion. They will end up costing too much.

DECISIVE COMPETITIVE ADVANTAGE

When marketing has done its job right, the company will enjoy decisive competitive advantages. It owns its turf. If a competitor sets foot on it, an aggressive marketing organization will be able to drive that intruder away.

The reason for segmenting the market and inventing complete products is to gain superiority in the market place. The device a company sells may not be particularly superior to the competition's. The device itself may be a little bit better technically or even slightly inferior when a customer closely examines the specifications, but the complete product will be so much better overall that no competitor can effectively challenge it.

Technical deficiencies, if they exist, can be overcome by superior distribution, better service and support, and a whole series of intangibles. Competitors will find themselves frustrated trying to overcome high levels of trust and long-term relationships.

The totality of what a leading supplier with a complete product does for his customer is so overwhelming that a few technical deficiencies will be overlooked. When companies offer complete products to a loyal customer base, the customer will be so satisfied with the product that alternatives will be evaluated with great reluctance. Even when a competitor comes up with a product offering that is in many ways more attractive, the customer will give the premier supplier the benefit of the doubt.

At the end of the battle for a market segment, the company having done the best job is entitled to a secure lead, a lead that will let it earn a fair return on its investment and then the chance to continue doing a superior job for the customer. It's a nice position to be in.

THE STRATEGIC PRINCIPLE

All that I have just said can be distilled into a single marketing maxim. To repeat:

Marketing must invent complete products and drive them to commanding positions in defensible market segments.

THREE

Slightly Better Is Dangerous

Announcing the newest breakthrough in personal computers from Upstart Systems! It uses the same microprocessor as the one used by IBM, but because of our clever technologists it runs just a little bit faster. The operating system is almost identical, and it runs faster too. Of course, it has lots of software. It uses most of the same programs supplied by the IBM. How big is it? Well, it has a smaller footprint than IBM's product—taking up 10 percent less space on your desk. Where can you buy it? Look for it at your nearest Upstart Systems dealer. To find him call 1–800–UPSTART. Incidentally, Upstart is 10 percent less expensive than IBM in its most popular system configuration.

W ITH THIS SALES PITCH as a magic flute, the Pied Pipers of the personal computer industry in the early 1980s rallied millions of dollars to their cause and led naïve investors, distributors, and corporate managements into a bloody war of attrition. Venture capitalists poured tens of millions of dollars into the cause. Some companies even became profitable enough to raise money in the public market. Corporate giants like AT&T, NCR, Xerox, Univac, Olivetti, ITT, and TI joined the chase. Large investments were made in product development, inventories, and marketing. Entrepreneurs raised money to start retail stores to sell the computer products.

Then, almost overnight, dozens of companies died. Scores of others were left crippled and doomed.

Why? Because the copies of the IBM PC that were only just a little bit better were not really better at all—not in the long term. Within months any advantages they possessed had evaporated. The price edge went away. IBM's newest products ran faster. And even the best of the new personal computers could not overcome IBM's real juggernaut, its brand image.

Incremental product differentiation is not the sole province of the PC business. A surprisingly large number of technology companies are capable of differentiating their products from competitors' by only the slightest of margins. There are lots of semiconductor products that are only a bit faster, or disc drives with slightly more capacity, or printers that are only a few dollars cheaper.

The most dangerous and quickest-vanishing of those distinctions is the last, lower price, particularly when born out of desperation and unsupported by lower costs. This advantage vanishes the instant a marketing manager, energized over the loss of an important order, directs the field sales force not to lose another order because of price. That usually precipitates what is known as "death spiral pricing."

By comparison, great companies are not just a *little* bit better in a few ways, they are *significantly* better in one or more ways that are important to the customer.

Most products inherently lack a significant edge. It is the job of marketing to create important differentials in products that are often little more than generic.

In marketing, I would much rather be significantly different than just a little bit better. That's because if you are different in an important way to a customer, you will be seen as significantly better as well.

But, mind you, it takes courage to be different.

I'm not advocating difference for its own sake. Nor am I espousing product rebellion. Rather, I am arguing for choosing a radically different strategy to better serve the needs of a group of customers.

At Intel we had a chance to make just such a move in our development system business. Shortly after we conceived of the development system business it became obvious to us that we were, in effect, entering a new segment of the electronic instrumentation business. After all, the device did a lot of the same things instruments did, only better. That meant if we were successful, the big instrumentation manufacturers like Hewlett-Packard and Tektronix would come after us.

Luckily, we had a fair idea what their strategy would be. Unluckily, they were certain what ours would be.

In essence, we wanted customers to buy development systems that worked only with Intel products. We wanted those customers to make massive capital investments in equipment dedicated exclusively to the Intel product line.

On the other hand, HP and Tektronix were going to build general-purpose equipment capable of supporting any manufacturer's microprocessor. Specifically, they were going to sell their general-purpose tools against our special-purpose ones. They were planning to become competent generalists and hoped to do a good job for everyone. They were going to offer the customer flexibility, freedom of choice—a good plan.

As the development systems business grew in importance at Intel, a few of us debated whether we should defend ourselves by entering the general-purpose business as well. For a number of reasons, we didn't. For one thing, it made no sense to provide easy exposure to our microprocessor customer base for our competitors. Opening up the development systems business would have done that. That, after all, was the business Intel was really interested in for the long term, even though for now the microprocessor business was smaller than the development systems business. However, this also made us sitting ducks. We obviously needed a strategy to counter the coming assault.

Our dilemma might seem a unique situation—that is, being constrained from entering a general-purpose market because we wanted to protect another business. But in truth it is not. Companies are constrained all the time for many different reasons. For example, if a big competitor is already in a market and doing a good job, that is a constraint, as most IBM-compatible PC manufacturers found out. But no matter what the reason for the constraint, if you can't win with a head-on assault, you'd better be prepared to be *different*.

The obvious alternative strategy for Intel was to pour all of its energy into becoming Intel product specialists. We did that in a number of ways. First, we got our new simulation devices to the market as much as a year before our competitors delivered theirs. We also offered the customer more software options. The quality of the software products for Intel components was better. Finally, and maybe most important, we supported our customers with application engineers who took total system responsibility. If the customer couldn't make the system work with our microprocessors, we fixed the problem. Our competitors lacked the knowledge to duplicate that level of support. We trained the customers simultaneously on the use of our microprocessor and our development system so they could get maximum use from both.

In short, we turned our specialization into an advantage. We trained our customers to see why it was better to be committed to Intel. We first convinced ourselves and then the customers that we could do a better job. We delivered on that promise.

Our customers voted for us with their dollars. Ultimately, they spent more than one-half billion dollars to do what was best for them—and Intel as well.

THE OBSESSION WITH DEVICE DIFFERENTIATION

Technology companies are often born from "breakthroughs." Thus they are usually preoccupied with the technical differences between devices. Marketing departments of those firms are frequently populated with engineers with little or no marketing training or sales experience. Their marketing experience is often overly influenced by what they think they once bought as engineers.

Standardization and the sheer complexity of technology have done much to make products look increasingly similar. Most 256,000-bit semiconductor RAMs nowadays are pretty much the same. If a brand name is not on the part, it takes a sophisticated test to tell one manufacturer's product from another. By the same token, there are a large number of computer systems based on the UNIX operating system. Technically, they are very similar. The list of examples could go on.

Now add to that the sheer complexity of the products themselves. It takes time to learn to use one. Even more hours are required to appreciate the subtle distinctions that make one product perform better than another. This book is being written on a PC using word processing software. The author looked at a number of software packages: Wordstar, Multi-Mate, Word, and DisplayWrite 2. I read a book on word processing and perused the manuals on two products. I talked with knowledgeable friends and got their opinions. Finally, I found a qualified salesperson and bought what she recommended.

Hours were spent in selecting the word processing software. Yet, the decision was not a rational one. And within a few weeks of using the system, I discovered many things I both liked and disliked about my choice. It would have taken me almost as long to make a similar evaluation of other products. Subsequent talks with users of other word processing products has exposed me to problems they are having with their products, easily solved by mine. Those users, frustrated by the inadequacies of their systems, did not know of the other solutions close at hand.

Product complexities make it easier to make products different, but they make it very hard for the customer to know that differences exist. And if the differences do not exist in the customer's mind, they do not exist in the market place.

As devices become more alike and at the same time incomprehensibly complex, then other characteristics differentiating products must become more important. That is precisely what is happening in the real world. With all semiconductor memories the same, customers are buying price, delivery, quality, and the relationship with supplier.

Word processing software programs are sufficiently incomprehensible to the casual shopper that he or she buys what is recommended by an expert. Thus the key ingredient in selling the product is not the software, or the manuals, or the training, but the direct relationship between the customer and the salesperson.

The preoccupation of many high-tech companies with "device" differentials is both costly and unproductive. Many inexperienced marketing people give up when the device proves not to be better than its competition. Instead of finding ways to turn the device into a better product, they ignore it and leave it to die.

DIFFERENTIATE PRODUCTS, NOT DEVICES

If the complexity of technology products makes it more difficult for customers to choose among competing devices, it can be a boon for marketing departments. To use an everyday example, think of the poor product manager for a plywood company. You must admit, it's pretty hard to make one board different from another. Yet the fact that customers have preferences means that they must be perceiving differences. Even prosaic little potatoes have differences. Frank Lamb, who runs a large corporate farm in Oregon, understands that. He sells his high-quality product principally to nearby volume customers to make french fries. The difference is not in the potato but in the location of the farm, the relationship with the customer, and the personality of the farmer.

Compared to plywood makers and potato farmers, the consumer marketeers have it easy. The lucky product manager who markets toothpaste has a wealth of available choices. He can flavor it with anything from scotch to mint, give it any color he dares, have it come from a tube with stripes, make it abrasive to whiten teeth, sprinkle it with fluoride, or deliver it through a pump.

That's only the beginning. What is conveyed about the product in ads and packaging is probably even more important than the toothpaste itself.

By comparison, high-tech is high risk. Here, the buyer is always concerned whether the system will arrive on time, whether it will work as specified, whether it can be properly applied, and whether the supplier will be able to fix it when it breaks. A high-tech buyer, more than most, will be biased to the supplier he or she believes will assure success. The intangibles are extremely important. IBM's reputation for support, HP's quality image, and Caterpillar's reputation for service are integral parts of their products. Those intangibles turn devices into products with perceived advantages.

Marketing always wants to be involved in planning the devices it will sell. It is fun to talk with the customers about their future needs and speculate about what engineers will be able to do. Oh yes, it's great fun to participate in the development of the next breakthrough.

Unfortunately, it's a lot easier to plan a breakthrough than it is to execute one. Remember, your competitors talk with customers too. And customers are more than happy to describe the same need to anyone willing to listen. That can lead several companies into trying to solve the same problem at the same time. Now, with several competitors in a race, there is the chance someone else will build a device very similar to the one you are planning or, worse yet, may engineer a better one. And, of course, there is the perpetual optimism that enables people to plan the difficult and do the impossible—but not on schedule or at the planned product cost. The graveyard for high-tech products is filled with devices that were great when planned, but came out late, cost too much, and were second best—in other words, devices that never became products.

At that point it is easy to blame the whole debacle on engineering and to let the product die. This is the time to remember the old maxim, "The trees have blemishes, but the forest is beautiful." The device may have flaws, but the product still can be great, if marketing does its job.

Intel had such an opportunity with the 8048 microcomputer. It was both an engineer's and a marketing person's dream. The product had everything. Best of all, it was stamped "Intel," the world's leading supplier of VLSI. Yes sir, the 8048 had everything going for it.

Except that it had fatal flaws as well.

Fairchild, a company that had never been in the microcomputer business, had a different view of the market. It defined a product, the 3870, which better fitted the high-volume needs of the companies making low-price products. Intel's 8048 was targeted at the high end applications of computer-type companies.

The key advantages of the Fairchild 3870 included four more input/output pins and a very low price. Faced with that competition, it became depressing even to make customer calls. Big deals were being lost everywhere in the world. Fortunately, the 8048 was truly different. In desperation, a marketing campaign was structured around the performance advantages of the 8048. A customer base was developed of firms that needed those differences, ones less sensitive to price and input/output pins. But still, Intel's sales were limited to low-volume computer-type accounts. Intel could never catch Fairchild at the volume accounts.

Companies committed to satisfying customer needs think first of the customer when designing new products. Only when the market segment is well understood can the product be tailored to the customer base. In all likelihood, the resulting finished product will be dramatically different from other products optimized for different customer bases.

That is what happened with the 8048. It was the perfect product for the customer base Intel best understood. The Fairchild 3870 was a better product for a larger market segment composed of firms manufacturing very high-volume products, the ones Fairchild understood. At first the differences between the two market segments were not understood by Intel. As a result we expended a lot of effort trying to sell the 8048 in places where it did not fit. Only when we understood the problem could the company focus its energy on the places where the "differences made a difference."

In much the same way, Apple's new Macintosh is trapped in its market segment. The computer conceived for "the rest of us" is designed to make it very easy for the first-time user to get started with the system. Through saturation advertising, the public now knows you don't need a lot of manuals to use the "Mac." You can instantly test-drive the system.

Apple's dedication to creating "the computer for the rest of us" led it to develop a unique product. Its desire to satisfy the needs of a market segment ultimately led to a generic "device" that was transformed into a significantly different "product." If most companies aimed their product definition efforts at satisfying the needs of unique groups of customers before they invented the device or service, their products would end up with many important characteristics that would clearly differentiate them. Technology companies have more flexibility to do that than others, such as those in the plywood, toothpaste, or potato business.

SALESPEOPLE MAKE A DIFFERENCE

Salespeople live by creating perceivable product differentials in the customer's mind. Since technology products are usually sold one-on-one, the salesperson becomes the ideal marketing vehicle. Salespeople are always interested in what their product can do that no other product can. Armed with such knowledge, the creative salesperson then nurtures a need within customers for that characteristic. If the product has a number of unique characteristics of great value to a customer, then the salesperson's job is that much easier. Unfortunately, most marketing departments don't do enough to educate their salespeople about what makes their products different. Salespeople are frequently told only specifications, not a product's true advantages and the benefits those advantages bestow upon the customer. Often the salespeople are left to discover for themselves what makes the product special. However that education takes place, a good salesperson determines what is important to the customer and then relates the important differences of the product in a fashion that makes those characteristics essential.

The greatest salespeople do not stop at the differences provided for them by their companies. They create differences. There was a brash and bright salesman in the 1960s who peddled semiconductors in trendy suits and drove racy cars. Many purchasing agents of the time loved the approach and wanted to buy from that unique individual. Today his old friends still flock to him and happily send in purchase orders. The clothes are more conservative now, and the car is a Rolls Royce. That salesman, Jerry Sanders, holds court as the president of a multi-million-dollar company, Advanced Micro Devices. He is still one of the world's greatest salesmen.

Sanders's edge was his image. It still is. He created a difference with which customers loved to identify, and that sold a lot of product.

AMD isn't the only great high-tech sales story. One clever instrumentation salesmen I knew discovered a very important service he could offer his government laboratory customers. He found the procurement procedures to be so complex that government engineers themselves did not understand them or have the time to deal with them. So the salesman decided to do his customers' job for them: He wrote the government's own specifications and did the internal paper work. Over the years he did that job so well that the government engineers trusted him to find out what their needs were and even to spend much of their own budgets for them with little supervision. That relationship lasted for years, because he was conscientious about never violating his customers' trust. As he loved to say, he was "careful never to buy them anything they didn't need." (On the other hand, I am unaware of any orders he placed for competitors' products.)

I once asked one of IBM's star salesmen what he did when the competition was 20 percent higher in performance and 20 percent lower in price. The reply was instant: "I sell myself. I tell the customer that he can only get me if he buys from IBM. I tell him I will personally insure his installation is a success."

Good salespeople make a difference. They are powerful tools for making your products and services unique when properly trained, and they can tailor the product to the customer. They can even become the product. Figuratively speaking, the customer buys the salesperson, and a physical device is shipped in that salesperson's place. That is why hiring a good salesperson away from a competitor can be so devastating. The acquisition of a salesperson is really the act of buying a piece of the competitor's product line—as well as carving out a chunk of its customer base.

DISTRIBUTION DIFFERENTIATES

Products reach customers in many ways. Customers are frequently more wedded to their distributors than to their suppliers. That is precisely why private labels and generic consumer products work so well. The reputation of the retail store stands behind the product, and in many cases that image is better than the brand image of the manufacturer.

Distribution can be a powerful differentiator. If a customer buys only from Hamilton-Avnet, then a product not carried by that distribution firm will not reach that market segment. If a product is sold only through discount chains, it will not reach the regular clientele of Neiman-Marcus.

The bottom line is this: Distribution channels are powerful differentiators and frequently own the customer, and if a company is going to reach that customer, it must figure out how to bias the distribution network in its favor.

That is an extremely difficult truth for many high-tech companies to accept. When the company has just finished work on the fastest, lowest-power, highest-noise-immunity device in the world, it is hard to believe that customers will buy the distributor and not the device. Yet that is frequently the case.

The power of industrial distribution channels can be seen in the clever marketing strategy developed in the early days of National Semiconductor by Don Valentine. At the time National was all but bankrupt and locked in competition with the giants of the industry. Valentine decided to use distributors exclusively to sell National's products. All orders, no matter how large, were taken through distribution. The policy was the exact opposite of the one used by National's competitors. It made National unique.

In the mid-1960s, when Valentine pursued that strategy, the environment in the semiconductor industry was very different from what it is today. Delivery schedules, which are still not great, were very unreliable then. Salespeople would frequently urge customers to place a portion of their business with distributors, who maintained local inventories, in order to make up for shortfalls from the manufacturer. National shared the same distributors with many of its competitors. In this environment, the fiercely competitive National prospered.

A distributor who feels positively about a supplier company can do a great deal to steer an order to that company. A distributor can quote better delivery on one product line than another or can offer better prices. It also can provide one supplier with superior intelligence about a customer, a real competitive advantage. In short, the distributor can make the product different.

Some of National's competitors at the time felt National got more than its fair share of business from distribution. On the other hand,

National felt it earned it. National kept its policy in place for a long time, even when it seemed to outsiders no longer to make economic sense.

As I write this, Compaq, struggling for success in the IBM PC–compatible market, is using distribution to differentiate itself. All computer retailers are concerned about the market power of IBM. For that reason, Compaq is committed to a policy similar to National's, that is, no business will be taken direct. It seems to be working: Retailers, struggling to reduce their dependence on IBM, push Compaq at every available opportunity.

Distribution channels frequently own the customer, just as salespeople do. Sometimes the brand image of a product is so strong that the distributor must sell what the customer demands. At other times the product is one-of-a-kind. Then the customer will demand it, and the distributor will have to sell it.

However, in many cases neither influence occurs. Then the service the distribution channel has given the customer and the relationship established over the years become the dominant considerations. The distributor, not the device, is the product purchased. Smart companies use that fact to their advantage and to make their products unique.

INTANGIBLES ARE BEST

The world of technology is one based on cold, hard logic and rational analysis—except where buyers are concerned. Consider the poor customer faced with a thousand pages of documentation and two weeks of training courses describing how to use a new system. Deluged with five competitive products and in information overload, it is hard to believe an objective evaluation is ever done.

Think of the engineer struggling to develop a next-generation electronic product. This innovator wants to take advantage of the most advanced technology, demanding the newest and best integrated circuits in his or her products to make them run faster and use less power. The circuits the innovator needs may still be on the drawing boards of the supplier. Thus the supplier is inventing circuits at the same time the customer is inventing the product. Obviously, the risks in such a project are tremendous. Development schedules on complex circuits frequently slip for months, quarters, even years. Yet companies are often driven to take such risks.

Ford Motor Company wanted to develop the world's best electronic carburation system for its cars. To accomplish that, Ford needed a very advanced microprocessor. A number of companies competed fiercely for Ford's business. Intel won the contract, not only because its device was superior but also because Intel's management got to know every key manager at Ford. Bob Noyce met Ford's then president, Lee Iacocca.

By the time Ford made its decision, the automaker not only felt good about the microprocessor, it felt great about Intel. Building confidence was a long and difficult process for Ford, but it had to be done. Put yourself in its position. Wouldn't you be careful if the millions of cars you produced were totally dependent on a twenty-dollar part?

To Ford, Intel's management commitment was an intangible factor. But it was enough in Ford's mind to be a significant differentiator. With technology products, intangibles can have an extremely strong influence on buyers.

The product of a first-rate jewelry store is not only beautiful creations but insurance. Customers are willing to spend more money knowing they aren't purchasing plastic jade or synthetic rubies. I expect my Maytag washing machine to last twenty years. No evaluation is needed. Even if Maytag's washing machine costs a lot more, I assume that the money saved on service over its life will offset the price difference. How do you overcome that kind of prejudice?

Marketing's job is to design intangibles into the product and then to use them to make products unique.

THE SERVICE JUGGERNAUT

As businesses mature, service to customers becomes increasingly important. It is one of the most significant ways commodity products are differentiated. As the capabilities of other types of high-tech products converge, one of the important surviving differences is the quality of service the company renders. But, as we shall see later, it is extremely difficult to give customers good service. It is almost as difficult to convince a customer you have it. That's why good service is such an extremely powerful differentiator.

Every company claims good service. Who wouldn't? The only response to that is to prove your good service with performance. Think of the salesman looking the customer in the eye and saying,

"Buy my hundred-thousand-dollar system and you will see that we have good postsale software support and can fix your system when it breaks." Now, compare that with: "You own five of our $120-thousand systems and they are serving you well. They almost never break down and when they do, we fix them promptly. We have trained your people and helped them apply the system, and we will do it in the future."

The Japanese are extremely service-conscious when it comes to their Japanese customers. The biggest customers get the right amounts of products and get them on time. If you are a favored Japanese customer, you have it made. If you aren't, you may find yourself sacrificed on the altar of loyal customer relationships. That's precisely what happened to many European and American customers during the 1981 semiconductor shortage. They were dropped by Japanese firms so they could support their most important Japanese customers.

How does a company convince a customer it provides good service? By delivering it year in and year out. That can be the most significant differentiator a company can have.

MAKE YOUR COMPANY DIFFERENT

As the intangibles become more important to the purchase of technology products, corporate image grows in meaning as well. Therefore, by making the company different, a marketing group can in turn make its products unique.

The importance of corporate culture has become better understood in recent years. Culture is important not only for a company's internal operation but for marketing departments and the customers as well. Culture establishes the tone of a company in the market place; it forms a part of the corporate image. It is just about impossible to be perceived as a service-oriented company and yet have a corporate culture that does not value service. Customers see through the fraud. Similarly, technology leadership is earned in the market by deeds, not by public relations. And technology prospers only in a culture that values it.

When a company is doing well, the press writes about its products, management, strategies, and culture. In that way the company culture is exposed to the outside world, becoming a part of its public image. It makes the company different.

Everyone knows what the names IBM, Neiman-Marcus, and

Hewlett-Packard stand for. Everyone understands the cultures and philosophies of those companies, and how those make their products different. All marketing has to do is create a preference for the corporate culture, and then the company will be "bought" and a device sold.

Lee Iacocca invented the New Chrysler Corporation and its culture. His product is pride in America and a claim that "the competition was good so we had to be better." Mr. Iacocca would have you believe a dollar spent with Chrysler is a dollar invested in the country's future. You can't buy that product anywhere else in the world, not from Nissan, Mercedes, Ford, or GM, and when you buy it from Chrysler, it throws in the car as well.

The company—its philosophy, culture, and what it stands for —are all part of the product the customer buys. The better the corporate image is, the better the product is. If the image differs from that of competitors in ways appealing to the customer, it is even better. The company will get purchase orders because of it.

PROMOTING THE DIFFERENCE

Advertising and public relations create some differences and communicate many more. In consumer products, the promotion is a significant part of the difference. When beer drinkers can't tell one beer from another in test after test, something must create the brand preference and make one seem to taste better than another. Springtime and romance are not in the perfume bottle advertised in a magazine; they exist only in the ad copy.

For high-technology products, the job of creating differentials through advertising is more difficult. After all, you can't create good product service with advertising. Leading people to expect it will exist when it doesn't will only undermine your reputation. On the other hand, promotions can do a great deal to make the market aware of company differences and advantages. When they are done in a skillful and forceful way, they can be extremely effective.

In the late 1970s the Japanese launched an assault on U.S. semiconductor manufacturers on the issue of quality. The blitz was complete, total, and most of all, effective. It wasn't long before customers blamed their quality problems on U.S.-made chips, in spite of the fact that many had extremely poor internal quality systems that were the source of the problem. The advertising and public relations effort mounted by the Japanese was superb. It took only a few short years for U.S. manufacturers to fix their quality problems, but the stigma still exists in many customers' minds.

For high-technology products, promotions seldom create differences by themselves. But when a good promotion is coupled with real product differentials, it is a powerful influence.

BEING DIFFERENT IS ALSO A SACRIFICE

If differences are a way of getting your company into a market, they are also a way of keeping your company out. The differences one company promotes are precisely the ones a competitor will frequently be able to use to exclude the other from a market. The purchasing agent wanting to buy off-spec parts does not call the premium-priced supplier. On the other hand, companies wanting to build reliable equipment don't talk with purveyors of "seconds."

For some reason, high-technology companies have a great deal of difficulty giving up a market. Consumer companies, in contrast, understand that this strategy is the very essence of success. Virginia Slims can't be made to appeal to males. The very differences that win some customers offend others.

Steve Jobs, the cult hero of the personal computer business, had a special rapport with young people, and he molded Apple's product to their needs. More than that, Jobs made Apple itself different. He was the hero saving the world from domination by the men in the gray suits. It all may sound absurd, but students and educators around the country bought that difference, and the Apple computers as well.

But that heroic image was not nearly so appealing to corporate America. Many of those companies, embarrassed by their problems and skewered in the same business press that extolled Jobs, not only were offended by the corporate position, they didn't buy Apples as well.

Differences are important in creating segment barriers. They are the factors that enable one company to do a superior job of satisfying the needs of one customer and beat its competitors to the order. But that success comes at a cost. The very barriers that keep competitors out of the market often can confine the victorious firm. One of Apple's problems is precisely that. The difference Jobs created is barring it from the business market. However, in such a velvet trap is precisely where a company should want to be.

51

Why? Because there is no choice. Be different or die. Establish your company's differences forcefully or someone else will establish them for you. Good marketing grabs the significant product differentials and makes them both big and important. It uses all the tools at its disposal: product features, people, service, advertising, distribution, corporate cultures, and company executives. When the job is done, the customers are bound to the company, because they have a preference for the difference.

FOUR

Why Companies Give Bad Service

Tom Peters, co-author of *In Search of Excellence,* commented in a recent training course at Hewlett-Packard that many corporations do not consider service a significant barrier to market entry. Unfortunately that statement is true, and it is as significant a condemnation of many companies as charges of poor product quality or inefficient manufacturing. Such a cavalier attitude toward service displays a chilling lack of understanding of one of the most serious problems facing businesses today. Service is poor in many service industries, abominable in many retail stores, and totally ignored by many technology companies.

For all, that is inexcusable, and in time those companies will pay for their indifference.

The newness associated with many technology companies and their product lines has shielded those firms from a service crisis. However, as industries mature, service becomes more important. Companies that have not yet put a service infrastructure in place will find it a long and expensive process. Frequently millions of dollars must be spent to repair the damage to the customer base and build the service organization—just at a time when the company can least afford the investment.

TRUE CONFESSIONS ABOUT
BAD SERVICE

Since I intend to pontificate throughout this chapter, it is only fair to begin with a confession about how I once gave horrible service and paid the price I have just described.

One reason I joined Intel in 1973 was that I had been promised responsibility for making design aids for customers who could use them to insert microprocessors into their products. I had thought about these design aids a great deal before I joined the company. I knew I could build them into a big and profitable business for Intel. I had talked with customers and knew they needed a new type of instrument, which ultimately would be called an in-circuit emulator (ICE). I knew if Intel could develop the ICE modules and put them in boxes called microcomputer development systems, we'd have a dynamic new business on our hands.

The ICE module was a revolutionary idea. It was the equivalent of an x-ray machine for microcomputer system engineers. They would use it to speed software and hardware debugging and to get products to the market faster.

At first no one at Intel believed in the idea. Software types didn't see why it was any better than software simulation tools. Engineers unfamiliar with programming couldn't see why anyone would buy it. Luckily Hap Walker, a creative engineer, became interested in the idea and developed a very clever solution for it. He is the inventor of ICE.

Ironically, in the end much of Intel's success in the microcomputer business was directly due to its success in the microcomputer development system business, that is, to ICE. Customers with our development systems could easily complete designs using Intel microprocessors.

We had a great thing going. We'd train customers at our training centers, sell them a development system to speed the design process, send in an application engineer to help with their application problems at the component or system level, and then sell them the microcomputer parts. We had a complete product and the best service and customer support in the industry.

Or so we thought.

When Intel first became interested in the development systems business, I had forecast that every dollar of development systems sold would annually generate about ten times as many dollars in component sales. The forecast had become a corporate joke. Soon the dollar sales of development systems had surpassed the sales of components, and everyone was wondering when, if ever, the tidal wave of component sales would flood in.

Within a short time development systems sales were approaching four hundred units a month, four times the original forecast. Customers loved the product. The hardware had been so well designed that it never broke down. Customers frequently could not remember when their machine had last failed.

That was pretty good luck for us, because if many products had broken we probably couldn't have fixed them. We lacked service technicians, spare parts, diagnostic programs, and maintenance procedures. In short, we had great product service because nothing ever broke.

Then we introduced a new version of the system. We had fifty of the new Series IIs running in the lab and were positive it was solid as a rock. We started shipping. Within days the phones were ringing off the hooks. By then we had passed the point of no return.

Systems were failing everywhere. The manuals were so inaccurate that if the customers followed them precisely the system would not work. The drop in humidity with the approach of winter made matters worse. The system was so sensitive to static electricity that a well-charged engineer could "electrocute" his or her program—"vaporize" might be a better term, because hours of work just vanished.

I learned two lessons about giving good service. The first was that *a service-oriented attitude will not assure good service.* Intel application and service engineers supported with bad logistic systems could not give customers good service no matter how hard they tried. The second lesson was that *if you eliminate the need for service, you are giving good service.* The prior high-quality product enabled Intel to keep customers happy despite a weak service organization.

The problem became so bad that Andy Grove asked Gordon Moore, chairman of the board, and Craig Barrett, director of components quality, to help me. There was no way such aid could be construed as a compliment to the management job I had done. With their support I began applying quick fixes to my problem. Pretty soon failure rates declined. The load on the service organization decreased, and it was better able to focus on the more serious problems.

After the battle was over, Intel embarked on a program to design quality into its system products. That was a big job, one not accomplished overnight. The first challenge was to create quality awareness throughout the organization. That took time. I ordered books on quality and distributed them. I walked the factory floor to talk with employees about quality problems. I spoke endlessly on the subject.

But the most important thing I did was send to management involved a memo with a defective wire harness stapled to it. The memos had an extraordinary shock effect. The factory had been fabricating this poorly engineered part for almost a year. The workers on the line knew it was bad and had complained, but no one would pay attention.

The memo did what the poor workers couldn't: It caused embarrassment. The problem was fixed immediately, and management was left with a reminder of its incompetence and insensitivity.

High product quality is the cornerstone of good service. For many companies putting good quality systems in place takes five to ten years, for others it takes forever.

But there was more to be done at Intel. My new service manager, Jim Grenier, understood that he lacked the service infrastructure to support his organization. Service documentation was poor. Training programs for his people were inadequate. The field organization lacked confidence in the ability of the factory to distribute spare parts, so it hoarded spares as insurance against shortages.

One day I audited a service office in New Jersey and found the manager had accumulated more than sixty spare floppy discs, ten times the number needed. Many of them did not work. He explained that if he sent them back, he might never see a spare floppy again. At least if he had them in the office, he reasoned, he had a chance of fixing them and servicing the customer.

Watching Grenier cope with those difficulties taught me the third important lesson about service: *A company has to have an infastructure in place if it is going to deliver good service.*

In Intel's case, putting the infrastructure in place wasn't easy. Training programs had to be improved. An on-line inventory system was needed to track spare parts in the field and factory. A service quality control organization had to be established to measure the effectiveness of the organization. Service engineering groups had to be formed within Intel operations to ensure that the equipment under design was easy to maintain. The list seemed endless, but Jim drove the organization and got the job done.

After years of hard work, Intel was once again capable of giving customers good service. I had learned three very important lessons. It took a few years more before I learned the final one.

Lesson four was that *giving good service was also a strategic problem*. I shall elaborate on that later in the chapter.

Of course, service problems are not unique to the computer industry. Take my new car, the so-called ultimate driving machine. I bought the car from a dealer who was proud of his service program. But it turns out that his organization can't deliver good service. The attitude of his people is good. They have fixed every warranty problem without so much as a question, even those costing hundreds of dollars.

The real problem is not attitude. It is the quality of the product and the dealer's and factory's logistics organizations. The dealer can't really predict how long it will take to make a repair, so I never believe the car will be ready when he says it will. Sometimes he doesn't fix the problem properly the first time. That may be a training problem (in spite of all the training diplomas on the wall), or it may be that the car just isn't serviceable. On top of that, it can take weeks to get parts, so repeat trips are often necessary.

We own another car. I can't tell you if the dealer who sold it to me gives good service or not. The car has never failed, and the dealer has only had to provide routine maintenance. Since the job is simple, it is always completed on time.

That's why building a product that never fails is the ultimate way to deliver good service.

SERVICEABILITY MUST BE DESIGNED INTO A PRODUCT

Companies cannot give good service to customers unless the service is integral to the product offering. The quality of the product must be planned to match the needs of the market. Total quality control defines "quality" with the words "fitness for use." That does not mean a product should last forever or never break. That would not only be impossible but would create unaffordable products. What it does mean is that a product should conform as well as possible to the uses for which it was intended. Any car will break down. The concept of total quality control would demand that the $10,000 car a company builds be the highest-quality $10,000 car that the company could profitably make and deliver the greatest level of satisfaction possible at that price.

The first mistake companies make in their service programs is selling products of inadequate quality. That only damages customer satisfaction. Further, a poor-quality product places tremendous stress on a service organization. After all, an efficient service organization is staffed on a statistical basis to service the average failure rate, with provisions for dealing with reasonably anticipated peak loads. Thus, all one has to do to devastate the group is to ship a product with ten times the normal failure rate. A moderate volume of such a product in customers' hands can easily double the load on a service organization—and suffocate it.

It is not only service technicians in the field who are overloaded when that happens. When complaints pour in, there are not enough people to answer the phones, the demand for spare parts goes out of sight, often the factory can't meet delivery schedules to support the normal demand and provide the spares, and the repair center becomes swamped with returned products.

Everyone knows how difficult it is to build a high-quality product, but good service starts with good product quality. How companies incapable of shipping quality products can conceive of service as an insignificant barrier to market entry is incomprehensible to me.

That said, it must be added that building a high-quality product is not enough. Serviceability must be designed into products in other ways. That is true not only for hardware products but for products of service industries as well. For example, computer companies offer a very important service. They sell updates to their software products. But if the software is not properly designed initially and if that design is not well documented, it becomes almost impossible to maintain it, fix the bugs, cleanly update it, and train the support staff.

Industry has not always been so concerned about serviceability. One American-made car had several spark plugs so inaccessible that the engine had to be taken off its mounts to change them. For many pieces of electronic equipment, it is still almost impossible to get at the power supply. In an age when equipment was simpler and skilled labor inexpensive and abundant, the public was less concerned with those problems. That is no longer the case.

Maintenance represents only one issue a company must grapple with if it is going to render good service. The performance of the manufacturing organization is equally crucial. Customers want products delivered on time. Reliable and accurate deliveries permit customers to reduce their inventory levels, saving companies millions of dollars in the cost of capital, administrative costs, scrap, and warehouse space.

But accurate deliveries are not enough. Many large customers want their products shipped continuously throughout the month. Factories, for various reasons, tend to produce a disproportionate amount of their output in the latter part of a month, so shipping linearly to customers is difficult. Further, many customers like to change their minds. That is especially true in the consumer business. If a new Walkman isn't selling well, Sony will suddenly stop buying components to build more. Everyone knows how fickle the consumer can be, so a supplier really can't blame Sony for production schedule changes. The forecasting records of companies in the automotive, video game, personal computer, and disc drive businesses aren't so great either. For that reason, more and more customers want to deal with flexible and adaptable suppliers. Those capabilities enable suppliers to give better service.

It is difficult to be a flexible supplier. The cycle times in your manufacturing area must be very short. If it takes six months to build a device, then the manufacturer is, by necessity, going to resist any quick change in production schedules. On the other hand, if the manufacturing process takes only four weeks, a great deal more flexibility is possible. (By the way, manufacturers have found that short throughputs actually reduce manufacturing costs, not increase them.)

A short throughput time isn't enough. The manufacturer's suppliers, too, must have short throughputs. After all, if a manufacturer is going to accommodate its customers' rapid changes, its own suppliers must do the same.

For many customers, more is required than manufacturing flexibility. In rapid growth industries, customers want their suppliers to add capacity hurriedly to meet changing needs. The company that has the resources and is capable of bringing new capacity on-line quickly enough will gain a distinct advantage over the competition.

The Japanese semiconductor industry has done an excellent job of structuring its factories to service the mercurial demands of customers. A great many Japanese customers are in very volatile businesses. One minute there are not enough VCRs, calculators, and watches, and the next minute there are too many. The intensely competitive nature of Japanese business means industry shakeouts are always occurring. Not surprisingly, Japanese customers want to deal with companies that can quickly ramp up capacity during a boom and shut off the flow when a downturn hits.

In this environment, the Japanese semiconductor industry has learned how to add capacity quickly. The Japanese have become notoriously good at building plants quickly and ramping up production. They have also organized their manufacturing programs to accelerate factory throughputs.

Many companies are just beginning to appreciate the intimate relationship between manufacturing throughput plus capacity addition and service. It is a very tough job to cut throughputs by a factor of two or three or to double the normal rate at which capacity is expanded. The service-oriented companies of the future will have to learn how.

Needless to say, manufacturing can do its job and a customer still wouldn't get good service. Good service requires good logistical systems. That is true for almost any industry, whether it builds devices, writes insurance, transports people on airplanes, or takes orders by mail. If a distributor can't tell a customer whether or not an ordered part is in inventory or if a supplier can't ship a product on time, good service cannot be rendered. An airline whose reservation systems constantly break down cannot do a good job, no matter how efficiently its planes take off and land. A manufacturer who can't model capacity to predict future availability accurately will never be viewed as a reliable service-oriented supplier.

Electronic distribution is an extremely service-oriented business. Here a clash of titans is taking place. Hamilton-Avnet, the leader in the market, is locked in a battle with Arrow Electronics. This fight is of particular interest because the logistic strategies of the two companies are so different. Those strategies lead to different product offerings. Hamilton believes customers want local inventory and same-day delivery, so Hamilton distributes its inventory widely at more than fifty nationwide locations.

Now, anyone who has ever managed inventory knows when it's spread around it is never where you want it. The parts always are in Cleveland when the customer is in Denver. Furthermore, when parts are in short supply, the profit-oriented general manager in Cleveland (whose bonus depends on gross margins) won't be anxious to ship his highest-profit item to a colleague in Denver.

But, somehow, Hamilton makes the system work, delivering what it calls Super Service. Most customers would agree.

Arrow thinks it has a better idea. Arrow argues that local inventory isn't necessary and is a logistical nightmare. By putting a great proportion of its inventory in a few central locations around the United States, Arrow maintains it can get the parts to the right place within forty-eight hours—overnight if necessary. Arrow even has data to prove it is out of stock less often on products than its competitors, including Hamilton. But central inventories have their own problems. For example, the local general manager wants to take personal care of his loyal customers. He can do that much better, especially in times of shortage, when the inventory is under his direct control. In spite of that, Arrow does a great job.

The future of both companies will be determined by the effectiveness of their logistic systems. Arrow will tell any supplier willing to listen that it delivers better customer service at a lower potential cost, and that Hamilton's systems are on the verge of falling apart. Hamilton will reply that Arrow really isn't doing all that well, and the centralized system can work only by ignoring the local market.

So here are two service-oriented businesses, vitally dependent on dramatically different logistical strategies.

Both Hamilton and Arrow find it extremely challenging to give good service and have invested millions in the process. It's too bad many companies think good service is just an attitudinal problem. They tend to view it as simple to fix and as easy to attain. They think all that is needed is a service-oriented attitude. But that's only the beginning. If a company is not structured to give good service and has not invested in the systems to deliver it, it will fail.

GOOD SERVICE IS A STRATEGIC PROBLEM

Complexity is the plague of service. The plague is spread by marketing people trying to make sure the customer gets what he or she wants, no matter how far-fetched. As companies attempt to meet customer needs, the pressures build to provide ancillary products. When an analysis is done of the product line and one finds a large percentage of the products generate almost none of the sales, the marketing department will argue that those secondary products are leverage items. The existence of the low-volume widget, they say, makes it possible to sell lots of other items.

That may be true, but it is also true that the hundreds of varieties of widgets get in the way of giving the customer good service. Each of those products must be forecast, documented, built, production-engineered, supported with applications information, and so on. The resources expended doing that are not available to support the really important products. The numerous secondary products gum up the service works.

That problem becomes especially acute in technology companies serving multiple market segments with the same product. Computer companies have been continually hurt by the problem of overextension. The generic hardware product is the same for almost all types of customers. To enter a new market one need only add a little software. But before you know it, the company has customers in a number of different markets and is supporting numerous low-volume software offerings. Before long the quality of service degenerates. The resources have been spread too thin.

One of the best ways to ensure simplicity in a product line is to focus on serving the needs of a handful of market segments rather than many. When that is done, fewer products and less support are required, and the quality of service rises to its proper level. By making a strategic decision about the number of markets a company will serve, the service level can be improved.

Many companies unwittingly plan poor service into their product lines. Others consciously plan good service. IBM, which is continually criticized for its lack of technological leadership, has done an excellent job of planning service into its product. The company has eschewed constant changes in technology, especially computer architectures, which would make it impossible to deliver good service. IBM also has sacrificed technology leadership to attain service leadership.

General Electric, when it embarked on its plan to have three different computer architectures for different performance segments of the market, chose to optimize the cost performance ratio it provided at the expense of customer service and support. It was a conscious strategic decision—and a disastrous one. The company could never have provided service equal to that which IBM could offer for its solitary 360 Series.

Daisy, a leading computer-aided engineering company, has a difficult strategic problem. Because of strategic decisions about product line evolution, the firm faces a crisis of multiple operating systems. Daisy has its own proprietary operating system, has announced it will support the industry standard UNIX, and is currently delivering IBM PCs equipped with a different operating system. Documentation, quality assurance, training, software integration problems, and customer support issues strain most companies dealing with one operating system. Daisy now has to deal with three.

Daisy, of course, is not the only company to face that type of problem. Intel, DEC, IBM, and many others have had to support more than one operating system. The key has been to build up enough volume in each product line to make that support affordable. It remains to be seen whether Daisy can do so.

For years the semiconductor industry shipped parts to customers in both plastic and ceramic packages. Both types of package will be used for years to come. In the 1970s many customers for volume products demanded ceramic packages, even though they cost a great deal more. The reason was that parts packaged in ceramic were more reliable.

The Japanese, in their unceasing effort to reduce manufacturing cost and simplify production, made a strategic decision. They worked very hard to perfect the plastic package. After a great deal of effort, they were able to make it so reliable that the need for ceramic parts in many applications simply evaporated. Customers benefited tremendously from that effort. Not only did they get less expensive parts, they also got better service. The supplier, able to reduce the complexity of its manufacturing process, could offer more accurate deliveries. Today almost all semiconductor companies produce the majority of their product lines in plastic. Customers love it.

Good service is the result of a good business strategy, a strategy that simplifies and focuses production and makes it easier and less expensive to deliver it to the customer. Some of the strategic decisions require great sacrifices. Unless companies are willing to make those sacrifices, they will never be able to meet the customers' needs.

SERVICE IS SEGMENTED

A domestic traveler wanting to fly from John F. Kennedy Airport to any other U.S. destination late in the afternoon probably shouldn't fly Pan Am. It's not that Pan Am doesn't care about arriving on time, it's that it can't serve two masters (market segments) well at the same time. To make the travelers arriving from Europe happy, Pan Am often must hold flights. The flights from Europe are frequently late. Even if Pan Am were perfect, it would still have little control over slowdowns at Heathrow and the headwinds across the Atlantic.

Pan Am's problems are not unique. Every airline using a hub city concept faces similar difficulties.

The same is true in electronics. The original equipment manufacturer (OEM) purchaser wants a different type of service from the end user. The end user for a computer system wants it fixed on location and fixed fast. An OEM purchaser for the same type of system wants to integrate it with its own equipment and then ship the finished product to the customer, so to it good service is spare parts at a reasonable cost and training so its service people can fix the equipment themselves.

The customer at a discount store is there to buy inexpensive commodity products. He or she knows beer, toys, and sporting goods, and understands that lots of well-dressed sales clerks cost a great deal of money. To this customer, good service is not a lot of people saying, "May I help you?"

On the other hand, the customers buying diamonds at Tiffany's or a fur coat at Neiman-Marcus have a different problem. Few understand much about what they are buying. Many can't tell a good diamond from an exceptional one or a good mink coat from an extraordinary one. In such a setting a good sales clerk educates the customer. A customer who is going to spend thousands of dollars wants to be reassured that he or she is making a well-considered decision.

Different market segments require different service offerings. Excellent service for one group of customers is worthless for another. You must plan your service for each distinct customer category to which you sell.

THE 80/20 RULE IS MISLEADING

People talk about the 80/20 rule as if it were some unassailable law of nature. The rule states that 80 percent of anything one does in marketing is invariably due to 20 percent of something else: 80 percent of the sales come from 20 percent of the products; 80 percent of the business comes from 20 percent of the customers; 80 percent of the revenues are generated by 20 percent of the sales force. Anyone who has spent time in marketing is convinced of the 80/20 rule—if only because it is invoked so often.

But even if the 80/20 rule is true in most instances, its blind application to a customer base will often lead to the wrong conclusion. That's because customer size defines the nature of the service required. A customer who buys $100 million worth of product a year needs not only more service than another spending just $100,000 but a different form of service as well.

Intel has approximately 2,500 customers accounting for about 70 percent of company sales. It sells to those customers directly. The remainder of the customer base, measured in the thousands, is served by a worldwide distribution network. Less than 5 percent of the direct customers make up 80 percent of Intel's direct sales, and the ten biggest customers account for about 30 percent of the corporation's billings. Intel has a number of customers purchasing more than $25 million a year from the company. The smallest direct customer spends less than $100,000 a year.

The demands of the mega-customers are quite different from those of the little ones. Specifically, the large, sophisticated customers want to form tight buyer–seller partnerships and enjoy the resulting advantages. For example, by establishing joint quality programs, the largest customers eliminate incoming inspection. Some want access to Intel's advanced plans. Since many big companies have long design cycles, this information is of great importance to them. It is of less importance to small companies with short design cycles. They can respond more quickly to new product offerings.

In addition, when a large company buys a sizable portion of a supplier's output, it becomes very interested in that supplier's capacity planning. There are instances in the semiconductor industry where entire plants have been built to meet the demands of just a few customers. Massive increases in capacity require lead times measured in years, as well as huge capital investments. Needless to say, if a supplier is going to invest tens of millions of dollars to meet the needs of one customer, a very special relationship between the two must develop, and that situation is not unique to the semiconductor business.

The very large customer has its own special problems. It can't place a $100-million order with just any company. After all, not every supplier will have the capacity to fill it.

Ultimately, large customers and large suppliers become interdependent. The industry term in vogue to describe the phenomenon is "co-destiny." In a relationship of co-destiny, the buyer and seller deal in an environment of trust and understanding. The managements of both companies know one another well. Plans are shared. Supply is guaranteed, as are purchase orders. Prices are fair. The supplier makes a profit, and the buyer gets its product at a competitive price. Sometimes in periods of short supply, the seller sells at below the market price; at other times, in periods of overcapacity, the buyer pays more. Above all, the relationship is long-term.

If all that sounds too idealistic, it may be. Nevertheless, it is unquestionably the direction in which relationships between large OEMs and their vendors are headed.

The reason for such an evolution is that large customers cannot obtain good service from an important supplier without the highest levels of cooperation and support. Customers have come to understand that suppliers are part of their manufacturing process. To do a good job, suppliers need the same consideration and information as the customer's employees.

But the cozy relationship comes at a cost. If the supplier is going to be taken into a customer's confidence, it can't play poker with capacity and prices. Instead, the supplier has to be committed to superb service at a fair price. Customers lose their flexibility as well.

As one looks at industry after industry, it is easy to find customers of different sizes requiring different types of service. Not all customers can use or deserve the highest level of service. For example, it takes a big investment on the part of both the buyer and the seller to support a co-destiny program. It would be ridiculous for a small customer to make such an investment and demand a similar one from a supplier. It would only raise prices and make the customer unattractive to the supplier.

Rendering good service to customers requires a careful analysis of the customer base and then implementation of a service strategy to match service to customer size and needs.

GOOD SERVICE STARTS AT THE TOP

It should be evident by now that delivering good service is a pretty tough problem. Yet marketing literature, filled with endless discussions about all the interesting problems a marketeer faces, contains little about service. If I've done my job, the reader should be convinced by now that service is not only a fascinating problem but a decisive one.

Certainly a company will never be able to deliver good service unless its own leadership believes in it. Companies have to invest in service and make tough strategic decisions in order to deliver it. Other corporate goals my have to be compromised. A company may have to invest in service on an older product instead of developing a new one. It may have to delay the introduction of a new device because the service program is not ready. A company may even have to forgo entering a new market because it cannot build the proper service structure. Those are tough choices.

Good service depends as well on employees. Those individuals must place a high priority on serving the customer, and they will never develop that attitude unless top management already has it. Until every single employee understands that the objective of the company is to serve the customer, the customer will never get the best the company can offer. If that conviction does not exist at the top, this will never happen.

IT IS DIFFICULT TO CATCH UP

When a high-tech company gets behind in technology, everyone in management knows the firm is in trouble. If the company is publicly held, the management can read of its failure on the financial page of the local newspaper and in the business press. But when the company gets behind in service, frequently no one even notices—except the customers, that is.

Customers will tolerate a great deal when there is no alternative. They will complain, but they will accept. Probably for that reason, the managements of some widely successful companies tend to view service as a second- or third-order problem. To many it is more important to invest in the next breakthrough than in servicing the last one. To others it is more important to worry about building manufacturing capacity than building service capacity. That might be the right strategy for a few weeks, months, or even years, but the battlefields of business are littered with companies killed by the ultimate weapon in a war of attrition: service technology.

Unwelcome as it may be, every industry matures. When that happens, products lose much of their differentiation. Customers have other alternatives.

Take instant photography. The alternative now to Polaroid is not only Kodak but also one-hour developers. Changes of this type have affected Xerox, Intel, DEC, and hundreds of others. The battleground has shifted, or has begun to shift, from technology to service.

Great warriors always have tried to pick their time and place for a battle. If they were businessmen today, Patton, Napoleon, Caesar, and Alexander the Great all would have chosen to stand their ground on service.

When a company gets behind in service, it is very hard to catch up. Technology companies frequently spend 10 percent of sales or more on R&D. This means that if the next generation of products is going to be serviceable, considerable resources of the company must be devoted to developing maintainable designs and preparing for their introduction into the market. That is not easy when the company is also trying to cope with the service sins of the past.

Those past failures create a considerable burden. As discussed earlier, a poorly designed product can create a service load five to ten times what it should be. On top of that, a missing support infrastructure can compromise a company's chance to cope with the problem. The service documentation can be missing. Perhaps there are no courses to train service technicians. Worst of all, the service technicians might not even be there. Those problems all have to be solved while the company is trying to get ready for new products.

When companies get behind in service, they stay there for a very long time, unless they vanish instead.

CUSTOMERS ARE GETTING SMARTER

For years high-tech customers were as casual about service as many of their suppliers. That is no longer the case. Customers have become increasingly aware of the necessity of good service and the cost of not having it.

The price of maintaining a piece of high-tech equipment typically runs 1 percent of the price of the item per month. The service bill over a five-year useful life is typically greater than 50 percent of the price of the equipment.

That's not all. When the equipment isn't working, the owner is not getting useful work, so maybe the factory won't meet its production schedule or the engineers won't finish a project on time. The cost of lost output or slipped development schedules can quickly outrun the cost of maintaining the equipment. Customers who have experienced such losses have come to understand the true cost of ownership.

Really sophisticated customers now concentrate on the service levels of their suppliers. Typically, the overhead on a dollar of material consumed in the manufacture of product is 20 to 40 percent. Customers are starting to appreciate that their suppliers, by providing good service, can have a considerable effect on that overhead cost. If a supplier delivers quality product reliably and on time, the manufacturer can operate with much lower inventory levels. If the paper work is accurate, the manufacturer saves administrative costs. In all, good service can save up to 10 percent of the purchase price, and that figure doesn't include the enormous cost of line shutdowns caused by an unreliable vendor. It is no surprise that sophisticated customers today evaluate both the price of the product and the savings due to good service.

It comes down to this: The time it takes your customer to learn the value of good service is much shorter than the time it will take you to put a good service in place. That means you'd better get started now. Your customers may get there first—and they will be slow to forgive your shortcomings.

BAD SERVICE COSTS MONEY, GOOD SERVICE EARNS IT

Too many technology companies are foolishly preoccupied with the cost of offering good service. Sure it costs a lot to put applications engineers in the field. It is also very expensive to develop the technical information and service aids required to maintain equipment adequately. Maintenance organizations inevitably lose money in the start-up phase. The investment in spare parts for inventory is high. The cost of developing a computerized order entry system is huge. All that is true. Good service costs money.

But businesses exist to *serve customers*. Few customers can obtain the full potential value from a product without good service. On top of that, customers will pay premiums for reliable suppliers. They will purchase maintenance contracts. Even more important, customers will ultimately give their purchase orders to your competitor if you can't get your service program together.

So, in the end, good service more than earns its way.

It is bad service that costs companies money and market share.

TOM PETERS WAS RIGHT

To summarize, good service is a significant barrier to market entry. Before a company can offer superior service, it must deliver a high-quality product. It must also have a proper infrastructure in place. Companies must make the proper strategic decisions as well, or they will never be capable of offering good service. The employees must believe in the importance of service and must place a high priority on offering it to customers. Most important, management must be committed and willing to sacrifice other corporate goals in order to offer good service.

Tom Peters was right. Good service is a barrier to market entry. Getting there isn't easy.

FIVE

Great Products Make Great Salespeople

T HIS IS A CHAPTER about sales and distribution channels. It does not deal with sales techniques, territory assignment, motivational techniques, and sales management. There are lots of books on those subjects already. Rather, I intend to talk about the gross mismanagement and waste that take place in the sales and distribution functions of many high-tech enterprises. This chapter concerns asking people to do the wrong things in the wrong place with the wrong tools.

Let me give you an example from my own career. I joined Hewlett-Packard Company in 1965 because the firm planned to enter the minicomputer business. I had worked the previous four years as a researcher with the General Electric Computer Department and was disillusioned with GE and its endless, futile head-on assaults on IBM.

I was delighted to learn a great company like HP was entering the computer business, particularly that it was going to do so with a 16-bit architecture, not 12 bits like DEC's computers or 20 bits like GE's. Sixteen bits (that is, each word of memory would be composed of sixteen parts) was right on the money, as I saw it. There was no way you could go wrong with that type of architecture—or so I thought.

When I arrived at HP, I was shocked to find the company's first computer, the 2116, an architectural disaster. There was no way the market would accept it. My marketing career was about to begin.

The top management at HP wanted to be in the computer business. It knew customers generated a lot of data with HP instruments and needed to analyze that data rapidly. What they needed was a computer tailored to their kind of data acquisition applications. The 2116 was ideal for the job. Customers could plug their instruments into the computer almost as easily as they could plug a lamp into an electric socket.

Hewlett-Packard even had the perfect program for entering the computer market. The firm had hardware and modular software designed to work with its instruments; a sales force that talked to the right customer base; a service organization that could fix the product; and finally, a superb image in its segment.

Unfortunately, few people in the computer group recognized those advantages. The computer "jocks" who had come to HP from other computer companies had no intention of selling the 2116 to the instrument customer base. They had made many important engineering compromises to get management off their backs, but now that the product was ready, they were going to move "iron." They were going to attack the mainstream computer industry. They planned to knock off the fledgling Digital Equipment Corporation and, after that, the world.

But there was a big problem with that strategy: Customers for "iron" bought for price/performance, for the greatest bang for the buck. The HP 2116, while beautifully designed for instrumentation applications, was not competitive in the "iron" business because of its awkward architecture.

At that point in HP's corporate history, the company was committed to the philosophy of one salesperson per customer. Most of the good computer customers were being handled by instrumentation salespeople. The sales force, at the division's insistence, had been augmented with a few computer specialists.

The division drove the sales force to sell volume deals to computer "iron" customers, and the sales force just wasn't "smart" enough. It lacked experienced professionals. As you might guess, sales didn't go too well, and the salespeople quickly began to sell products for other HP divisions, the ones that told them they were good at what they did and didn't call them incompetent.

Meanwhile, this "dumb" sales force was learning something very important about the 2116, something so profound no one in the division could believe it was true. The sales force discovered some of its problems were a result not only of its own ineptness but also of a system that was too inefficient, too large, too slow, too cumbersome at input/output, and too expensive to compete in the "iron" market.

So there I was, a Ph.D. in electrical engineering with no marketing experience, sitting right in the middle of a big mess. The computer jocks kept seeing the big orders go to DEC and Data General, and they demanded that I, the new 2116 product manager, fix the problem. The field, on the other hand, had decided the only real market for the product was HP's traditional customer base.

The division marketing manager, an instrumentation guy, did not know what to do. I certainly did not. I didn't know then about market segmentation or training salespeople. I actually believed the proper way to train salespeople was to teach them about the product's physical characteristics, not what it did for the customer. I didn't know how to run a product crusade. All I knew was that we were failing.

Then a funny thing happened. We started to get orders—not from where we had been telling the field to sell the 2116, but from the traditional customer base. Things began to look up.

In time we even began selling the 2116 to mainstream computer customers. But the traditional HP sales force still wanted little to do with the new customer base, the "iron" buyers. Giving big discounts wounded their pride. They were suspicious of both the product and the new customers. Sometimes I would go into the field to close a big deal and would find that the field management wanted nothing to do with the sale. It was almost as if the division had been blacklisted by the sales force.

Shortly thereafter I became the marketing manager of the division, and I was called upon to negotiate two very big (for those days) computer deals, one for $500,000 and another for $5 million. I had never negotiated a big contract before in my life. Both were highly competitive and involved large discounts—and giving big discounts was an anathema to HP.

The salespeople and I closed both sales without the support of the field managers. Neither executive wanted anything to do with our sales. In fact, I was subsequently chewed out for "giving away the store," which I probably did. But on the other hand, I got the sale.

By then more real computer salesmen had been added in the field to develop computer accounts. It was a good idea, but it created an enormous new problem. It was a problem I never could solve, and for years after I left the company HP still struggled with it.

The problem was this: A computer could be sold by a HP computer salesperson only if that computer was not attached to any HP instrumentation. If it was, the instrument salesperson was supposed to get the sales credit. That arrangement was beautiful for the competition. Here were HP salespeople hooking HP computers to competitors' instruments just so they could get credit for the sale. And there were HP instrumentation salespeople hiding valid computer deals from the computer people out of fear that the latter would mess up other deals with the customer.

Experience has taught me that the ''gray'' area problem is not new. Lots of companies have figured out how to deal with it, using a number of different techniques. One thing is certain: the problem does not get solved when the field is fighting the factory.

Needless to say, I learned a lot of things from my experience with the 2116. The first and most important was that *giving the wrong sales force the wrong direction is a formula for disaster.* Compelling a sales force expert in serving one particular customer base to serve a different one is difficult and usually unproductive. If you must do it, you'd better have a good product, not a 2116.

Further, if the factory and the field had really lined up together and gone after the instrumentation customer base, HP would have gained a lot of momentum in the market. Instead, the groups worked at cross-purposes. When all was said and done, whatever success HP had with the 2116 was not the result of a great computer but because HP offered an adequate product to a traditional customer base its sales force controlled.

I am sorry to say my experiences of the late 1960s are not unique. In the fifteen or so years since then I have observed the same problem over and over again. I have found most factory groups really don't understand what the field sales force does or is good at. I have also learned that most field organizations are too rigid and too unwilling to try new approaches to new markets. Most important, I have learned that when the field and the factory are at war with each other, it is symptomatic of a serious management problem. It doesn't matter who is right in the matter. Management must find out what the problems are and solve them fast.

There is no doubt in my mind that sales and distribution are the least effectively used resource in most high-tech companies. Those companies frequently spend from 10 to 20 percent of their revenue on direct sales. Distribution costs range from 15 to 50 percent of the final sales price. Much of that money is misused. It is not only that companies could spend less and still sell as much, but the value of the missed opportunities is enormous. Waste half the time of your distribution and sales resources, and company sales will be cut almost in half. This, sadly, is precisely what many new product marketing programs do.

Remember the Apple Lisa? It was the high-end personal computer that was going to revolutionize business. Instead, it was a double failure for Apple. Apple not only lost its investment, but Lisa wasted the time and resources of Apple's distribution channels. The retailers invested in Lisa inventory, training salesmen, and advertising—for nothing in return. A great many of those dollars and a great deal of the effort could have been spent selling other Apple products. Instead, those sales were lost, possibly forever. Distribution channels were weakened by the failure of Lisa.

Giving a distribution channel the wrong product to sell to the wrong customer causes very great damage. Blame always seems to fall on the sales force and on distributors "too stupid and incompetent" to sell the product. Well, I for one have always been amazed at just how smart salespeople really are. It shouldn't be surprising. After all, they have the best teachers: the customers themselves. Salespeople learn very quickly about being asked to do the job in the wrong place, at the wrong time, with the wrong support. I am always surprised at how long it takes the factory to understand what the market is telling it through the sales organization.

KNOW WHAT SALES AND DISTRIBUTION CHANNELS DO

One can't help but be awed at the different ways products reach customers. Think about buying a watch. You can purchase one through a number of different retail channels, including discount jewelers, full-price jewelers, drug stores, supermarkets, sports stores, department stores, or mail order catalogs, and get them through promotional giveaways.

The watches themselves reach the retailer through a number of distribution channels. They can come directly from the factory, through a master distributor, or via a local distributor.

Even products with comparatively small market universes, such as semiconductors, end up with much more complex distribution patterns than one might imagine. Semiconductors are sold factory direct to customers by sales forces and sales representative organizations. In addition, about 30 percent of the product reaches customers through franchised distributors.

And that does not tell the whole story. A significant number of semiconductors flow through unauthorized distribution channels, bought from organizations with too much inventory and by companies claiming to be OEMs but acting as unauthorized distributors. Sometimes parts are supplied to those unauthorized channels with full knowledge of the manufacturer, sold on the spot market below market price (when there is an abundance) or above the manufacturer's suggested price (when there is a shortage).

For most businesses the distribution channels become incredibly complex. Many companies never completely comprehend all the ways their own products and the products of their competitors reach the customer base. If you don't understand all the distribution channels for your product and what function they perform, you may be missing a very important opportunity. Worse yet, you may be the victim of a successful attack on your company's product line by a competitor using a distribution channel you don't know about or understand.

Whenever a healthy distribution channel exists for an extended period of time, it does so because it fulfills a need. It may be serving a unique market segment, or it may be a different way of reaching your customer. One thing is sure, the channel is capturing market share for someone. It is adding value to a product for some customer; otherwise it wouldn't exist for very long.

I do not mean to imply a company should use all the channels available to it. That would create havoc and make the company's product unappealing to its most important distribution channels. When overdistribution occurs, because either too many different types of channels or too many similar ones are used, a company loses, not gains, market share. What is important is to understand the options available and to select the right ones. Those decisions should be continually reviewed, because markets evolve and distribution channels are constantly in flux, responding to market change.

It took me a very long time to understand that the word "distributor" tells very little about what that business does. While it should be self-evident, it certainly isn't to most people. Otherwise they wouldn't expect distributors to do so many things they can't or be so disappointed when they don't. No one would be shocked if a semi-conductor manufacturer couldn't build computer systems in its wafer fabrication area, yet many are perpetually surprised by the failure of a distribution channel to sell to a new customer base.

Nothing more exemplifies this confusion than the microcomputer system business. Some distributors merely deliver products with what has come to be termed "yoyo" (you're on your own) support. They sell on the basis of price and delivery. Other distributors sell only to retailers. They provide credit, support, and training so the sub-distributors can effectively resell the product to end users. Still others add value to the product before resale by providing specialized soft-ware packages, customer training, and other services. Some distributors understand data communications, some networking, and others, industrial applications. Some distributors offer only hard-ware, others only software.

The mere ability of a distributor to handle a generic product does not mean it is capable of selling that product to a multitude of diverse markets. As a matter of fact, the distributor may be capable of reaching only very select groups of customers. What that means is that you, the manufacturer, must understand the customer your distributor covers. Geographic coverage in no way guarantees that the targeted customer base in that area will be reached. Distribution is complete only when it provides both geographic and market segment coverage.

The same is true for direct sales channels. Not all salespersons perform the same function—nor should they. Similarly, salespersons are capable of serving only a limited number of markets well. They reach their peak when they deal with only a few market segments. Companies must decide what functions they want their sales forces to perform. It requires a great deal more thought than the trite formula: "Sell product."

The sales force of a technology leader performs a different function from the sales force of a follower. Intel's sales force was organized to do the market development required by a technology leader. It was structured to capture design wins by influencing engineers to use our products. The sales force was composed primarily of degreed engineers who understood computers and logic design. They were supported by technical experts capable of giving engineering assistance to customers applying Intel's new technology. Their principal job was to design new products into new applications.

The companies who second-sourced (copied) Intel's products did not spend much time with the engineers. They focused their attention on purchasing agents. They tried to win orders on the basis of personal relationships, price, delivery, and service. It doesn't take an engineering degree to make that sales presentation to purchasing agents, most of whom are nontechnical. As a matter of fact, many of Intel's salespeople didn't like working with purchasing all that much. When an account evolved to the commodity buying mentality, we frequently switched the salespeople on the accounts from the young, technically oriented hotshots to the older, more service-oriented salespersons.

Diversity in sales is not unique to semiconductors. In some industries salespeople don't call on the customer. In the ethical drug business they inform the doctor and service the pharmacist. They don't call on the patient. For many consumer products salespeople service the distribution channels and fight for shelf space. In many of those cases the product is presold to the customer by advertising, packaging, and retail presence.

There are myriad functions performed by sales and distribution channels. Salespeople don't all do the same types of things in the same industry, and they perform vastly different functions, in different industries. The same is true for distributors. Companies should give a great deal of thought to what they want their sales and distributor channels to do. Once they decide, they should make sure those channels are doing that job.

If you think this is obvious, you may have a problem. A surprisingly large number of technology companies have never thought through the issue. What's worse, they are paying to have the wrong job done.

SALES AND DISTRIBUTION CHANNELS ARE SPECIALIZED

Sales and distribution channels are specialized, not generalized. One should not confuse the capacity to do a generic job with the skill required to do a specific one.

Any competent distributor of commodity products must have the ability to provide its customers with rapid and timely delivery. For that, the distributor must have in place the logistical systems needed to manage inventory and process orders. But that doesn't mean a distributor can effectively distribute any product. Not only may it lack contact with the right customer base, but when it is unprepared for the specific goods, the simplest problems can become nightmares. For example, some of Intel's distributors lacked the ability to handle and store large, heavy packages when Intel entered into the system business. Their inability to handle heavy items caused them great inconvenience, resulted in injuries to warehouse personnel, and often led to damaged equipment.

Equally, while any direct sales force should possess rudimentary and general selling skills—like those taught in basic training courses applicable to salespersons working everywhere from insurance companies to computer manufacturers—no computer firm would ever hire the world's best life insurance salesperson and ask him or her instantly to go out and sell mainframes. Certainly that individual is a great salesperson. But he or she lacks the necessary product knowledge and the specific sales skills to operate effectively in the computer sales environment.

Properly run, a good direct sales force is a finely tuned organization, superior to the competition in serving market segments. Salespeople know their customer base. Long-term relationships have been developed with customers and can be called upon for favors and information. The salespeople know and understand their customers' problems and in turn can present the features of their own product line in a manner that best offers a solution. Above all, the sales force is good at taking care of its customers. It has established a relationship and created trust.

That care shows in many ways. Credit policies, contracts, and other business policies are tailored to customer needs. Inventory is stocked in the right places and in the right amounts to give customers timely delivery. Quality assurance programs are set up to guarantee the customer defect-free product.

A similar degree of sophistication can be achieved in distribution as well. A good distributor structures itself to serve distinct market segments. Within those segments, the good distributors offer a full line of products not only to maximize their sales efficiency but to be more useful to customers. Thus a distributor selling computers to businesses would carry complementary hardware lines, such as printers and terminals, as well as the right cables to connect them, and frequently used supplies. Specialization is a key to a distributor's success.

People who have tried to change the final destination of a sales channel find that it is a very tough job. When a company takes an existing sales channel and tries to use it to attack a different market segment, it frequently finds the job far more difficult and expensive than planned. No hospital would order its staff of neurosurgeons to retrain for cardiac bypass surgery because it wanted to develop a new market, yet the equivalent happens all the time to sales forces in business.

The direction of a sales channel can be changed, and new market segments can be added, but it takes money and time, and the result is often inefficient. The cost of redirecting a salesperson toward an unfamiliar and dramatically different market segment is approximately 50 percent of the cost of maintaining him or her in the field for a year. In many businesses that can add up to 5 percent of the targeted sales. For example, if a company wishes to sell $20 million in a new market segment, it should be prepared to bear a refocusing bill from the sales force of $1 million. Unfortunately, product plans seldom comprehend that cost.

Surprisingly, even distributors and sales forces don't seem particularly sensitive to the problem during initial planning phases. One reason is blind enthusiasm. Aggressive sales and distribution organizations love new challenges. Furthermore, those organizations are often jaded by all the services and support they currently enjoy.

Products evolve and markets change, so sales and distribution channels are in perpetual flux. They must evolve or fail. The crucial point is not that sales channels shouldn't change but that a large investment in time and money must be made to effect the changes. New skills must be learned, much of them by trial and error.

It is always interesting to watch a factory group during such a transition. It usually believes it has discovered some new wisdom only it possesses and can't understand why the field sales force is so slow to learn the obvious. In fact, the sales force usually isn't that dumb at all. Rather, it is the first to learn the world does not function in quite the same way as the factory envisioned it.

Once the shift in sales channels has begun, new relationships must be formed. Often a new sales support structure must be developed. The geographic distribution of the new market segment may be different from the old one. That means new sales offices. The after-sale support for the new customer base may also be much heavier than in the past. That means more applications engineers. In short, the specialized channel that was effective for one product line and one market segment may not work for another without substantial modification.

The problem becomes more acute as the market segments become more distinct. In such cases the existing sales channels may be of little or no value at all. They may not even be capable of serving as a basis for the new channels. Then the challenge becomes one of building an entirely new distribution system.

Few companies understand the specialized nature of their sales and distribution channels. Companies fail to comprehend what the channels are really good at and how much knowledge, training, time, and support was required to make them effective. As a result they underutilize the resource, frequently misapply it, and assume they can transform it with ease.

SUPPORTING SALES AND DISTRIBUTION CHANNELS

A sales force is the corporate army. Its mission is to assault competitive strongholds, defend the company's turf from attacks by the enemy, gather intelligence, and capture new territory. The weapons it uses are product knowledge, customer knowledge, price, service, persuasion, and support. Just like any army, it will be effective only if provided with training, logistic support, and the proper equipment.

One of the most important jobs of marketing departments is to make products easy to sell. They do so by providing the sales force with the proper training and sales aids and by preparing the market for the product with the use of advertising, public relations, literature, and conference presentations, and by working with industry groups. If products are easy to sell, sales productivity improves, and most salespeople, who are usually compensated by incentive schemes, will devote their efforts to them.

If a marketing department is going to make a product easy to sell, it must understand what a sales force and distributors do, the skills they possess, those they need to acquire, and how they spend their time.

Remarkably, many marketing departments think they know but don't understand. Frequently technology marketing groups are populated with bright young people with little or no field experience. As a consequence factory-designed programs often miss the mark. The sales aids often solve the wrong problems; the application notes are not applicable to the real world; the administrative policies get in the way of the sale; and training doesn't really focus on the right issues.

A well-designed marketing program comprehends every step of

the sales process and facilitates the big ones. Good sales training explains how to qualify customers and the persuasive arguments that should be used. Answers to customer objections are provided. Application engineers are trained to provide assistance on the most commonly encountered problems, and application notes document the solution to many of them. Price quotations are developed in a timely fashion, as is delivery information. Products are delivered when promised.

It is an extremely difficult job to support the sales and distribution channels in a way that makes them truly effective. One reason marketing and general management should spend time in the field is that it is the best way to learn if the company is doing a good job. You can learn a lot about the quality of your sales support while listening to a salesperson on a long drive to see an important account. You can find out a lot about the effectiveness of sales training and sales aids over a dinner table. I, for one, was always surprised by what I heard. For example, in one geographic area the price quotations always arrived quickly from the factory groups. In another they did not. Some divisions understood the current pricing environment and others never did. Delivery information from some groups was accurate, and from others it was lousy. Some regions worked well with distributors, and others alienated them.

A salesperson, whether he or she works for a distributor or for the factory, is just like the rest of us. His or her most valuable resource is time. For most products, sales are directly proportional to the productive time the salespeople spend selling. Factory groups are doing a good job when they increase the amount of time the salespeople spend in front of the customers and provide the salespeople with the tools to make the time effective.

IT'S NOT A PRODUCT WITHOUT
A DISTRIBUTION CHANNEL

A new device or invention will never become a product without proper distribution. The device itself may have the potential to address the needs of many customers, but without specialists to put it in the hands of those customer segments, it will not succeed. When the right product is properly matched to the customer base and a specialized sales force and distribution channels are added to it, the result can be a tremendous success.

Too often the channels are matched to a market segment but the product isn't. (That is especially true in the computer business, where just a little extra software can make the sale.) In such cases the sales force is reduced to playing repairman, fixing the product to match the customer base. It may even have to acquire software for the customer. While that may be a satisfactory approach for very small markets, when the application is broad the result can be a piecemeal attack by the field.

The typical scenario will show an incomplete product introduced and failing to live up to the manufacturer's expectations. Pressure is placed on the field. In response, the field sales force struggles to tailor the product to the customer need. Suddenly, fifty field sales offices are working in parallel to make the product fit. One couldn't pick a less efficient way to do business. The problem is especially pernicious because the waste of resources is not obvious: It occurs in the field, hundreds of miles from the home office.

This underscores one of the great maxims of business waste: There are never enough resources to do the job once at headquarters, but ten times as much energy can be wasted in the field and no one will bat an eyelash.

Often high-tech companies come up with devices that serve market segments with which the distribution channels have no contact. The resulting sales are quite disappointing. Frequently companies don't understand why. The reason is the sales force seldom, if ever, talks to the new customer base, and then only ineffectively. If the sales force sells only in New Hampshire and all the customers are in Vermont, you get very few sales. If the distribution channels serve only one group of customers in a geographic area, and that group doesn't need the new device, the results are the same.

A device can never be a product without distribution, and not just any distribution. Sales and distribution channels can transform the device into a product only if they serve the right market segment.

PRODUCTS ARE SOLD THROUGH DISTRIBUTION, NOT TO DISTRIBUTION

For years the semiconductor industry took credit for sales to its distributors. At the same time semiconductor firms protected those inventories with rebates when prices dropped. When prices fell, companies had to credit their distributors with some of the difference on the products remaining in inventory. Since abundant supply was required tó drive the prices down, the market always collapsed at the very moment inventories were highest. So manufacturers frequently took a double hit: a drop in volume due to inventory buildup in the channel, and a large credit against sales to distributors on products that never reached the customer.

One company, Signetics, so wanted to delay that kind of sales reversal and prop up its earnings that it held distribution prices high long after the market broke. The result was a catastrophic loss of market share.

High-tech companies have a history of storing their sales in distribution channels and then ignoring the fact that those products really haven't been sold. Texas Instruments did so three times: with watches, calculators, and home computers. TI wasn't alone. Most personal computer manufacturers have experienced the false prosperity of taking profits on unsold inventory.

The way to prove to distributors or retail chains that you have little comprehension of their function is to call them "customers." While it is true that those organizations do order products, they do not buy them for the same reason as customers do. Customers purchase products to use them. Distributors obtain products to pass them along to those customers. The needs of the two groups are totally different. For that reason, distributors need a special kind of help.

"Help" for distributors means education, promotional tools, and effective policies to enable them to prosper as they sell. Without those things few distributors can succeed—and remember, when distributors fail they frequently take their suppliers with them.

No product is ever really sold until a customer consumes or uses it and derives utility from it. Unused products are sometimes scrapped, but more often they are returned or sold as surplus. The flow of unconsumed products is extremely fluid; it usually comes back to haunt the supplier.

Most distributors slant their expertise toward the customers to whom they sell rather than toward the products themselves. Thus, they are quite dependent upon suppliers to provide them with technical information and support. Distributors handle many product lines, spreading their expertise very thin. This "market basket" approach is an efficient situation. It cuts the cost of distributing and servicing the small customer, because the selling and support expense is spread over a large sales volume. It's convenient for the customer as well, since it reduces the number of suppliers the customer must deal with.

A distributor may have just one person responsible for marketing a product line. A manufacturer, in contrast, may have a hundred. But even with such a preponderance of corporate resources, it is remarkable how little is done for distributors—and how much is expected of them. There is a great deal of leverage to be gained by providing distributors with the support that makes your product easy to sell. Sometimes even the smallest effort on the part of a manufacturer can mobilize a large and potent force in the market place. The smartest companies put in place programs that ensure the success of distribution.

It is a lot easier to add distributors and channels of distribution than it is to make them effective. Nowhere is that better illustrated than in small business computers. In this industry, companies added dealer after dealer without adequately training or supporting them. As a result, both the manufacturers and the dealers were losers. Weak dealers took up manufacturers' time and produced no results. The unsupported and unhappy customers the dealers left in their wake in turn destroyed the reputations of the manufacturers.

Companies always seem to add distribution channels and assume some magic will take place. They naïvely believe that adding a distributor is equivalent to adding an effective distribution channel. In high technology that is not the case. The distributor is only as effective as the support it receives. If the company fails to provide it, the channel will frequently fail. The product may be stored in the warehouse, but it won't be sold to the customer.

THE HIDDEN COST OF DISTRIBUTION

When it comes to sales and distribution, few companies get what they pay for. Over time, as products mature, such channels can become very efficient. But in high-tech, by the time the channels have matured, the product is often obsolete or the customer will have changed. So the learning cycle must start all over again.

Large amounts of money are often wasted on distributor margins. A distributor can be doing the wrong thing (or nothing), and the situation won't be discovered for months. That is because the distributor is one step removed from the factory, the communication lines more tenuous, and understanding less complete. On top of that, many distributors won't protest loudly about being overcompensated. Thus companies and customers often pay to support distributor margins and may get very little in return.

In many instances it is not the distributor's fault. After all, distributors handle broad product lines. They cannot be expected to be intimately familiar with the details and the markets for every product. What they do know they learn over time from the market and the supplier.

Time and again companies, enthusiastic about new products, try to provide marketing direction to distributors. Distributors in turn frequently act on that advice, usually because they wish to maintain a good relationship with the supplier. But their efforts are often very unsatisfactory, as the supplier frequently doesn't understand the job to be done and misdirects the distributor.

That is precisely what happened in the early days of the microprocessor business. Semiconductor companies competing with Intel found they did not have the resources to develop all of the smaller accounts, so they sent their electronic distributors on a wild goose chase by encouraging them to call on design engineers and to buy nearly useless development system equipment. They never adequately trained the distributors to do the job. On top of that the distributor employees weren't all that trainable. They lacked the proper background. For the most part the suppliers did not know how to sell to the designers either, so the blind were leading the blind. As a result, distributors invested millions in equipment and wasted a large amount of sales resources attempting to do a job they were not prepared to do.

Don't ever kid yourself: Distribution is tremendously expensive. Electronic distributors often operate with margins of 25 percent. System distributors typically require 40 percent margins to run a profitable business. Technology companies looking at those numbers have a very difficult time reconciling the margin with the value they receive. But the cost of doing business is also very high. Distributors frequently earn less than 5 percent gross on margins on sales. So the issue is not one of overcompensating the distributor but of getting what you pay for.

In electronics distribution, distributors spend large amounts of money on inventory, service, materials handling, warehousing, order processing, and customer billing. Their operations are structured so that they perform those functions extremely well with small customers. But attempts to use the same channels for large customers or for equipment not requiring all of those services can lead to considerable waste. That happened to Intel with one system product.

The devices were sold through distributors because essentially all of Intel's products were sold through distribution. Customers understood that Intel encouraged placing small purchase orders with its distributors. Customers placed the systems, initially selling for about $10,000, into the small purchase category. Try as Intel might to discourage the sale of development system products through the distributor channel and to sell them directly, it was never able to do so. Customers wanted to buy the product that way. Distributors wanted to sell it, especially since it was so intimately tied to the follow-on sale of components. All rational attempts to correct the problem seemed to lead to a great deal of friction between the company and the distributors. Intel did not want to alienate them, because too much future components business depended on the distributors' good will.

Neither the customer nor Intel, nor even the distributor, derived much benefit from the whole arrangement. In the first place, the instrumentation business (the development system was an instrument) had never used this form of distribution, primarily because it was not needed. Customers did not need overnight delivery of the systems, hence distributor inventories of ninety days made little sense. Shipping heavy equipment to central locations for transshipment to customers just added to an already expensive freight bill.

Nevertheless, the distributors spent a lot of money on those services for the customer, and though Intel put a large margin in the price to cover the cost it was still not enough to make the distributors happy. How could Intel? It was competing with other instrument companies who did not use this expensive channel, because the customers did not demand it of them.

That is a perfect example of using a channel of distribution to do the wrong job. The customer got less service from Intel because margin dollars were spent on electronic distribution instead of direct technical support. The customer paid about 20 percent more for a lot of services supplied by the distributor from which he got little utility. On top of it all, the distributor felt exploited because the margins were inadequate. They were too small. He couldn't run a profitable business on them.

While this is a gross example of doing things wrong, the waste was probably no larger than in many other cases where distributors are picked to sell products that really don't fit the customer bases they serve.

One small computer company, Durango Systems, tried to get its dealers who dealt in the general business market to sell a specialized system to insurance brokers. The results were disastrous. The salespeople didn't feel comfortable with the application and were ineffective. In the few cases where systems were actually sold, customers were unhappy with the inexpert installation. Durango wasted a lot of energy and resources supporting a channel that simply could not do the job.

A company will never get what it pays for from distribution if it asks it to do a job for which it is poorly prepared and uses a channel that offers the wrong services. The money and effort are wasted.

USE A SPECIALIST TO DO A SPECIALIZED JOB

Lots of things can go wrong in the management of sales and distribution functions. Certainly there will never be a simple solution to all the problems. However, the failure of companies to recognize the specialized nature of these organizations is the root cause of many of the difficulties. That lack of understanding results in companies trying to use the wrong channel, spending too much money to distribute a product, and, worst of all, losing sales. The careers of specialists, asked to do the wrong job, are wasted.

Even when the right channels are chosen, they are frequently used inefficiently. Companies do not provide sales and distribution with the tools and training to do the job right. Sometimes, of course, no correct channel exists at all, and a company has to build one. Then the investment and support costs skyrocket.

By picking the right channel to do the job and supporting it in the proper fashion, companies add one of the most critical elements required to complete any product. If only companies would ask what specialized skills the sales and distribution channels require before planning to use them, much of the wasted effort could be saved.

Companies should design programs to make sales and distribution channels experts at selling their products to targeted market segments. If they did this before they plunged ahead, they would avoid many of the serious mistakes others have made.

SIX

Great Promotions
Are Simple

G REAT PROMOTIONS are acts of creativity, insight, and brilliance. But they are more than that. They are also acts of great leadership. Brilliant copy, striking ads, and dramatic press releases do not create products. Rather, they enhance what is already there. Great promotions become interwoven into the fabric of a company; they not only augment the product but reflect the corporate strategy as well. They tell a story about both the product and the institution it represents.

Contrary to myth, great promotions do not begin in smoke-filled rooms with corporate executives in animated conversation with copywriters, creative directors, and PR persons. Rather, they are conceived in the market place. They derive from a clear understanding of customer needs and emerge into the world as words. Initially, the words may be tortured, but with hours of long work they become great copy—copy that expresses, with eloquent simplicity, the focal point of the promotion; copy that inspires customers and employees to act; copy that provides leadership; and copy that captures people's hearts, minds, and imaginations.

Do things like this really happen? You bet. You don't have to look far for examples. The world's greatest copywriters are found not in ad agencies but in the capitals of nations and on the battlefields. Some of them have written words like, "I shall return," "The only thing we have to fear is fear itself," and "I have nothing to offer but blood, toil, tears, and sweat." Those words positioned the product and inspired the commitment of millions to carry out very distasteful tasks, even to give up their own lives.

Other inspired copywriters, when faced with events of lesser proportion but of comparable significance to their own institutions, have come up with such phrases as, "We're only number 2, we try harder," "The computer for the rest of us," and "The best made, best built cars in America." Like the words of MacArthur, Roosevelt, and Churchill, those expressions live on. They change the behavior of customers, as well as the actions of the corporations that use them.

But ad copy works only when it is backed by substance, commitment, and leadership. Robert Townsend, the president of Avis, believed in the "We try harder" campaign and led Avis to live up to its claims. Customers loved it. Lee Iacocca renovated Chrysler in order to deliver on his promises. Those promotions were more than just words. They were expressions of purpose.

Not every product is backed by the company president, the prime minister, or the five-star general, but almost every product has a product manager whose duty is to become that product's champion. The great "little" promotions are waged by those unknown crusaders. If those individuals didn't exist, neither would most successful products.

CUSTOMER BENEFITS GIVE BIRTH TO GREAT PROMOTIONS

Not everything that goes wrong in high-tech marketing is the fault of bad advertising or PR, but you may be convinced it is, to hear some marketing people tell it. Actually, bad advertising and PR programs are usually not the fault of the people who devised them. If the underlying message is not sound in the first place, no amount of brilliant ad copy or publicity can save it.

Nevertheless, when things go wrong there is a tendency to call in the advertising and PR agencies and demand a quick fix, a brilliant idea that will cure the problem. The ideas that emerge from these sessions are usually mediocre and make little if any contribution toward that goal. The problem is always the same: The substance is lacking. That is not to say promotions can't shape events. They can. But for high-tech products (and many others) promotions can't change reality.

In consumer products, promotions have a great deal more to do with shaping the product. They can affect popular tastes and create fads. They can actually imbue a device with qualities that customers find desirable. By showing great athletes drinking Lite Beer, the promotion can provide susceptible consumers with an identification with their heroes. It can make drinking Lite Beer a macho act.

A good promotion captures the essence of a product and makes it appealing to customers. It initiates the buying process. A good promotion also galvanizes the company or groups within the supplier to sell the product. Surprisingly enough, the underlying message of a promotion may not be visible to the customer. The Crush campaign at Intel was an internal effort rather than an external one. Fed up with being beaten by Motorola, the company decided to fight back. The word "Crush" never appeared in an ad. It was, however, etched in the mind of every salesperson, executive, and marketing expert at Intel. Before long the word "Crush" took on an internal meaning at Intel similar to "I shall return."

For most products, good promotions begin with marketing people succinctly expressing the benefits a product will bestow on a distinct market segment. While that discipline is common in consumer marketing people, it is frequently overlooked in high-tech. Possibly that results from a lack of training, but more likely it is inherent in the technological orientation of the companies. Too many think of their businesses in terms of the devices they manufacture rather than the benefits those products provide to customers.

But no matter what the reason, a shockingly large number of promotions are started without an understanding either of the customer or of the product's true benefits. When that happens, any chance of success is reduced to luck.

BE PERCEIVED AS YOU REALLY ARE

In 1969 Jack Trout introduced the world to *product positioning*. For the next decade advertising and PR groups were preoccupied with this new concept.

There was good reason. Positioning is a very powerful concept. When used effectively, it can provide tremendous guidance in promoting a product.

Regis McKenna has his own definition for positioning:

Positioning is a psychological location in the consumer's mind, pertaining to the relative qualities a company, product, or service may have with respect to its competition.

The position a company wants to occupy must be well thought out. A company should have a clear idea of how it wants to be perceived. It must also face the fact that wishes are not always feasible. The world will not see a company as a technology leader if it can't demonstrate that capability. Nor will the company be seen as a high-volume supplier of products if it cannot consistently meet the volume needs of the customer base. Corporate positions must reflect both reality and reasonable aspirations.

Even if a company makes no attempt to position itself, it will become positioned in the market—usually by the competition or the press. In a particular industry or market only one company can wear the title of "the technology leader." If a competitor takes and holds that position, it is no longer available. There is, of course, the opportunity to be the company that is almost as good, but nobody wants that position. Similarly, there is room for only one service leader and only one leader in volume production. A lot of other competition may be good, but not the best.

The positioning process starts by determining the most desirable perceptions customers can have of a company. Different market segments will value certain characteristics more than others. A company will want to be perceived in terms of the things most valuable to its customers. Of course, that is not always possible; a company may not possess those characteristics and may have little prospect of acquiring them. In that case it is sometimes better to change the market segment than to try to change the company.

Such situations are often encountered in the computer industry. Companies constantly head out with great aspirations to become suppliers to a broad market. After experiencing severe setbacks and loss of credibility, they fall back on tight vertical markets where they can best meet the needs of the customer base.

Over time companies develop expertises and products with particular attributes. For example, one company can support its products effectively, but in the process so burdens the product introduction cycle it can't offer customers price/performance leadership. Another company can't support its products very well but always leads the market in price/performance. Customers recognize those differences, so it is senseless for the company with weak support to try to claim to be a service leader, or the one with poor price/performance to sell a nonexistent feature.

Companies are always complaining that all the good positions are gone. That is especially true when there are a few very strong competitors in the market. The big guys always seem to grab the most desirable images and leave the dregs for everyone else. But all this really means is that lesser companies have bought their more successful competitor's claims or are attacking the wrong market. Furthermore, technology companies tend to sell their customers short. Enamored of technology, they discount other powerful reasons why customers might want to buy their equipment.

I recently visited a small computer company whose sales had been stalled for a number of months. The firm had merchandised a number of items but had consistently missed a big promotional opportunity. The firm had been caught in the trap of trying to take a position every one of its competitors wanted as well.

Meanwhile, the chairman of the company had found, in spite of the company's problems, that customers were still buying the firm's computers out of respect for the quality of its software people. What a wonderful way to position a computer company! Most computer customers know that the quality of the supplier's people is the most important ingredient required for the generation of quality software. The company had a great opportunity to sell computers by informing customers about this valuable resource. Customers had already granted that position to the company, so the image would be easy to build upon. Furthermore, as almost everyone else in the industry was pitching performance and was trying to establish that position, this was a terrific way to be different. On top of that, the quality of the software group is intangible, and intangibles make for great market positions.

As Alvin Toffler wrote in *Future Shock*:

> One of the curious facts about production in all the techno-societies today, and especially in the United States, is that goods are increasingly designed to yield psychological "extras" for the customer. The manufacturer adds a "psychic load" to his basic product, and the consumer gladly pays for this intangible benefit.

With a proper plan of communication, the computer company

could have metaphorically loaded its computers with its software quality reputation. After all, that is no different from IBM's shipping the image of assured success with its computers.

Good positioning depends not only on what the company wants but on what the customer demands as well. Things work best when the two coincide, and if a company has a consistent strategy, they will. When a company's strategy is inconsistent with customer perceptions, it might be better off to swallow its pride and select the image its customers pick for it, provided it is positive. That is what occurred at Intel. The company always wanted customers to see the 8086 in terms of performance. Customers, on the other hand, bought the system because of its software and its applicability to the office environment. Finally, we acceded to our customers' desires. Things worked better.

Those divergences of opinion shouldn't happen. When they do, they provide evidence that a problem exists.

The "New" Chrysler Corporation occupies a consistent position in the hearts and minds of Americans. It is a superlative example of consistent product positioning, corporate positioning, and Iacocca positioning. The customer knows when buying a Chrysler that he or she is buying a commitment to quality and performance, a piece of the American dream, the opportunity to support beleaguered American workers, and a chance to cheer for a cult hero. Those are great positions, because the ads say so, the president of the company says so, and the employees of the company are committed to them. Furthermore, the American public wants Chrysler to have that position. It wants a winner as much as Iacocca and his employees do.

Not every product can have an American cult hero as its champion. The company president might not even know the product exists. However, if that product is going to attain its full potential, it must find a champion, someone willing to wage a *product crusade,* as Townsend and Iacocca did. It is the job of marketing to supply the corporation with talented people to perform this function.

Few companies are so structured that product and corporate positioning dovetail neatly, but a corporate position can and should form an umbrella over the products. For example, the companies of Transamerica Corporation are all supposed to offer "first-rate service at a fair price." If the corporate position is going to work, the various products subsidiaries offer must support that position. Intel is committed to being a technology leader. While it is not always possible with so many competitors trying to do similar things, every Intel project attempts in some way to meet the corporate goal.

The positioning of a technology product is not merely a fabrication of the ad agency and the marketing department. Rather, a position is an outgrowth of the market being served. It must be designed into the product. The new product must exemplify the company's philosophical beliefs about itself and its products.

In an earlier chapter I discussed the problem of giving customers good service. To expand on that: No company can deliver good service merely through good copy. The service infrastructure and strategy have to be there from the beginning, and quality must already be designed into the product. Only a corporate commitment to service will enable a company to position itself as a service leader. More important, a company must deliver good service for years before it can claim that position. Companies delivering service in their ads and not in reality often negatively position themselves by raising, then disappointing, customer expectations.

The essence of good marketing is the commitment to be something. But remember one thing: You cannot hold two divergent positions at one time. A company can't be both the premium-price supplier and a price slasher. A company can't be a supplier of low-priced watches through drugstores and offer the same brand of watches through Tiffany's. Strong positions bind companies to markets and customers to companies. Good positions ultimately exclude companies from supplying market segments. Therefore positions must be picked with extreme care.

Strong positions are not easily attained. They must exist in fact before they can be made to exist in the mind. Nor can positions be earned by a brief flurry of activity. They are achieved through campaigns: an advertising campaign, a PR campaign, and a corporate campaign. Positions are won not by a single event but by a stream of consistent events occurring over an extended time. Positioning requires consistency at every point of contact between company and customer. Every employee who talks to a customer or the press should understand the need and substantiate the company's positions. When they do, it does not take long to see momentum building. Consistency is quickly sensed.

By definition, every company and every product will have a position. After all, the position is nothing more than the perception a customer has of the company and its products. The real issue is this: Will the position ascribed to the company be a result of aggressive effort that reflects positively on the company and creates demand for its products? Marketing's job is to make sure that happens.

SIMPLICITY WINS

Everyone remembers what MacArthur said. Everyone old enough knows what position Avis held in the rental car business and what it was going to do about it. Customers are sure when they go to Wendy's that they can find the beef. It hangs over the edges of the bun. For those unsure of their computer competence, IBM offers the little tramp, the world's greatest incompetent, to introduce the PC. When the little tramp achieves success, there can be little doubt you can do the same thing.

The ideas expressed in each of those promotions are not complex. They are simple, logical, and appealing statements—ideas the customer will remember. Even when the copy is forgotten, the concepts will still endure.

The sheer complexity of technology products is often a trap. Time and again a high-tech company will try to tell its customers everything about its complicated product in a single promotion. The resulting copy is impenetrable, the headlines are long and arcane, and the graphics are incomprehensible.

It is always easier to tell a lot about a product than to tell just a little. But simplicity is the key. If it were toothpaste, the task would be much easier. After all, how much can you say about clean teeth, cavities, and bad breath? But, the truth is that the people who make the toothpaste have the same problems as the ones who make the computers. Their product may do it all too, but they can't say everything they want to in their ads either.

When the Japanese assaulted the dynamic RAM-type memory chip market in the United States, they used a very simple message. Japan Inc. told customers it was selling price, quality, and delivery. It was. The customers remembered the message, and the promotion worked. Japan made deep inroads into its American competition. When Intel introduced the 80186, the product could do a lot of things, but the one that single device did best was to replace fourteen integrated circuits and save the customer money as well. It was easy to structure the promotion around that message. When we did, the field sales force instantly understood what it had to sell, and the customers knew what they wanted to buy. The product was a great success.

That message worked well because it was easy to understand. The customer could remember the message and then pass it on to a friend. Equally important, the message was so simple and compelling that everyone in the company could understand it. That meant that anywhere a customer touched the organization, he or she would get the same clear response. That was usually enough to convince that customer that the company could deliver on its promises.

Promotions must be memorable. That is why repetition is important. Repetition is hard for any technology company to attain. The reason is that most technology products sell in relatively low volumes. In addition, advertising and promotion budgets typically run 1 to 3 percent of sales—insufficient to reach a customer base with a sustained program.

There is also pressure to fragment promotional messages, particularly in companies with broad and complex product lines. There are so many products and so many benefits to describe that the company overloads customers with too many messages and details about too many products. Instead of running a few ads with interlocking messages, companies get trapped into unrelated, overly dense, limited-run advertising campaigns.

That is why positioning is so important to promotion. The process focuses the attention of the company on one main point. A company may in time run many ads and talk to the press on numerous topics, but as far as is possible each of those communications should support the basic position.

If a product line has strategic integrity and a company has a commitment to a specific set of goals, and if the corporation is focused on a well-defined market segment, the company's communications and promotions will, of necessity, support a basic position.

Businessland, the Neiman-Marcus of computer retailing, positions itself as "the place where business people are going to buy computers." That positioning works not only because business people need a place to shop but because it accurately reflects Businessland's focus. Its salespeople are professionals and better qualified to discuss business applications with prospective customers than most of its competitors. The products carried in the store are well suited to business applications. Further, the stores themselves are located near business centers, not in retail malls filled with children.

From the name of the store to the copy in the ads, Businessland's message is told again and again in many different ways. The company's product satisfies the customer's needs. Customers remember the simple message.

When a company's product line is fragmented, when its strategy is unfocused, and when its market segments have little in common, the job becomes infinitely more difficult. Businessland is committed to

100 percent company-owned stores, each implementing the same strategy and policies and carrying the same product lines. It competes with other companies, notably Computerland outlets, which are franchised stores.

Because they are franchised, the markets served by different Computerland stores are varied. For example, some stores sell products aimed at the home and children. Others don't. Thus the product lines carried by Computerland stores differ. There is a great disparity in the ability of stores to support customers. But Computerland does satisfy people's need for computers.

Because of the fragmented structure of Computerland's business, it is difficult for that firm to transmit the type of simple substantive message that Businessland does. Computerland therefore subsists by telling customers that it is the biggest. The customer benefit associated with that message is somewhat obscure. Besides, the company has difficulty tailoring its advertising to the customer base. The market segments are just too diverse.

Great promotions depend upon the transmission of simple and well-articulated ideas in a repetitive fashion to the market place. They depend not only on the creative concepts developed in the marketing department but on the focus of the corporation. If promotions are to be both simple and forceful, they must be backed by a unified corporate philosophy.

GOOD ADVERTISING AND PR ARE AFTERTHOUGHTS

Everyone wants to start a promotional campaign with an advertisement and a press tour. Why not? It's fun to do creative work. It's exciting to see one's name in print.

But that is the wrong place to begin. The great promotional campaigns are always outgrowths of what already exists. They have their roots in the market segments being served, in the corporate and product position, and in the corporate focus and strategy. One of the most frequent problems faced by business people trying to create promotions is that their corporation lacks those elements.

On the other hand, if a corporation has cultivated those factors, good promotions are simply extensions of already existing ideas. The messages to be transmitted are commonly known long before the marketing department ever meets with the ad and PR agencies. The audience being addressed is clearly identified. The discussions around the table focus not on *what* should be said but on *how* to say it and *how* best to reach the customer.

Unfortunately, few creative sessions go that way. If they did, there would be fewer ulcers among advertising executives. Creative sessions too often are an occasion for people to indulge in repairing the corporate and product façade, applying verbal putty to cracks in the company's image, not to discovering ways to communicate the company's essence.

PROMOTION IS PART OF A PROCESS

The goal of a promotion is to sell the public on the company and its products. Promotions use a number of vehicles to contact and influence the target audience. They include sales calls, ads, articles, direct mail, seminars, and trade shows. Great promotions extend over long periods of time, some for years. The reason consumers know Bufferin will not irritate their stomachs is that they have heard the same claim for years and have confirmed that claim through use.

The environment where a great promotion is taking place is exciting. The employees believe in the message and want to tell the world. Some develop an almost religious conviction about the program. That's why the substance of the program is so important. The convictions making a promotion a success can't survive on hype alone.

In consumer marketing great promotions sell a large percentage of the products. They create the "pull." When the customer walks into the store, the advertising has already all but closed the sale. For many lower-priced products, the salesperson or clerk merely accepts the customer's money. Even with many of the higher-priced products, customers enter the retail outlets with their minds already made up. A good number of automobiles are bought on television; the price is merely negotiated in the showroom.

The situation is very different for most high-tech products. Their complexity is often so great that an advertisement can tell only a portion of the story. It can inform a customer about a new product, but rarely can it offer sufficient information to make the sale. Customers wanting more information are usually provided with articles, manuals (which can be hundreds of pages long), application notes, catalogs, and brochures. That can be extremely expensive.

One of the most effective selling techniques for high-tech products is to get potential customers to attend a seminar. At such functions companies can hold the customer's undivided attention for hours, even days. IBM has used the technique for years. Intel used traveling road shows in public facilities or, when possible, in customers' plants.

For high-tech products, the selling process is part of the product promotion process. During it the customer will see ads, read manuals, talk to salesmen and distributors, attend seminars, tour plants, receive demonstrations, and visit with company executives. That means there are also many opportunities for the customer to receive conflicting messages about the product and the company selling it. Maintaining consistency throughout the process is a difficult challenge.

Here again, clearly communicated product and corporate positions are key. When every employee understands the message he or she must transmit, the stream of events can proceed smoothly. If the product position is established early in the life cycle of the product—preferably when development begins—the literature and promotional materials can be developed to support the position properly. When positions are developed too late in the cycle, on the other hand, chaos can result. Since the information content of technology products is very high, a lot of money is spent on manuals, sales literature, seminars, and demonstrations. There is seldom enough money or resources to do the job twice. If consistency is not established from the beginning, the customer will probably be barraged with contradictory messages contained in the different media.

Promotions are programs of great complexity taking place over extended periods of time. They are not short sprints or high-energy/high-creativity output sessions. They are creations of good management. Great promotions depend on clearly articulated positions and a systematic approach to communicating those positions coherently in everything the company does. For technology products it is an extremely complex process.

GREAT PROMOTIONS ARE ACTS OF INSPIRED LEADERSHIP

In all of the material I have read on advertising and promotions, the issue of leadership has never been addressed. Yet that is the very heart of the matter. Leaders, whether they are generals, prime ministers, corporate presidents, marketing managers, or product managers, inspire their "markets" to act in response to a message. The public cannot be forced to respond, it can only be motivated to take action. It may be led, but only with the proper tools. That's where positioning comes in. Creating the position and determining who the real customer is and why he buys are the most difficult parts of any promotion. The rest flows with relative ease. When this foundation is in place, the leader can then head the charge, and competent ad and PR agencies will find creative ways to communicate it.

SEVEN

Price on Value but Charge
What the Market Will Bear

PRICING IS one of the most important functions a marketing department performs. When prices are set too high, products never fully develop their markets, leaving pockets of opportunity for competition. When prices are set too low, the company gives away thousands, if not millions, of dollars in profits needed to finance its future.

For all that, pricing decisions are often based on only a fraction of the necessary information. What's more, many high-tech companies have little understanding of what information they need to make a prudent pricing decision.

Pricing is an art. Analysis, while helpful, gives only the probable right choice. In fact, the impact of a pricing decision, good or bad, usually is not fully understood until it is too late. That is best illustrated by the unintended consequences of two pricing decisions made during my tenure at Intel.

The first really powerful 8-bit microprocessor on the market was Intel's 8080. It had been preceded by a lower-performance device, the 8008, which initially sold for $36. Since the 8080 had ten times the performance of the 8008 and was probably hundreds of times more useful, I decided the market would, initially, be willing to pay ten times the price. Intel easily sold out every 8080 it could make. We recovered the total development cost of the product in the first two months it was available.

A good pricing decision, right? Wrong! Many customers decided the price of the 8080 would remain high for a long time and so delayed any decision to design the 8080 into their products. In fact, the $360 price was etched so deeply in the customers' minds that it was extremely difficult to erase. That gave Intel's competitors, the late entrants into the market, a chance to capture a lot of designs that should have been ours. Yet this obvious problem was never forcefully raised during any of the long discussions at Intel on pricing the 8080. The irony was that the 8080 ultimately sold for just *two dollars*.

So much for "charging what the market will bear."

Most companies, however, learn from their mistakes. A few years later Intel made a dramatically different pricing decision. As noted earlier, the 80186 was conceived as a product that would displace approximately fourteen other highly complex integrated circuits. The only problem was that as the design progressed, the chip grew in size, which made the cost of the circuit skyrocket. Ultimately the projected manufacturing cost of the 80186 exceeded the combined market price of the fourteen devices it was going to replace. To say everyone at Intel was depressed about the future of this product would be a gross understatement.

As you might expect, there was considerable debate about how to price the 80186. Some wanted to keep the price high until the circuit could be redesigned and the costs reduced. Others wanted to lowball it, reasoning that there was a brief window to capture designs. I was the main proponent of this point of view. We believed that by the time the customer's designs went into production, the cost problems would be solved—or so we hoped.

Finally a decision was made to price the circuit at $29.95 in volume. That was approximately the price of the fourteen integrated circuits it replaced and about one-half its initial cost. The product was aggressively merchandised. Design wins soon were pouring in beyond Intel's wildest dreams. The product became so popular, in fact, that many customers used it for applications Intel had never imagined.

A great pricing decision, right? Wrong again. The decision was a poor one, not because Intel couldn't ultimately make any money at that price, but because the company didn't have sufficient capacity to seize the opportunity. Worse yet, as Intel was the only supplier of the

80186, many customers had to delay, cancel, or curtail programs using the product. The antagonism created in the customer base was horrible to behold.

The 80186 pricing decision was made in the middle of the great semiconductor recession of 1982. Capacity was an issue farthest from executive minds. Even if it had been considered, no one had much faith in the product anyway. Predicting a capacity shortage on such a long shot would have earned derision.

Even very experienced people make lots of wrong pricing decisions. They are among the toughest a company makes.

ARE PRICES AND COSTS REALLY RELATED?

Prices and costs are related, but not nearly as directly as people think. Obviously businesses won't sell below cost for very long.

When a marketing department is given cost information about a product, it will tend to rely heavily on that information in determining the value of the product to a customer. I've long believed the first pass at pricing a product should be made without foreknowledge of what the product will cost to manufacture. When a marketing department knows the cost and the margin acceptable to the company, it will use those data to determine a price acceptable to the company rather than to the market.

That is a lazy and naïve approach. If you are interested in finding out if your company is guilty of pricing by computation, try this experiment. Deprive your marketing department of cost information during a pricing exercise and see how much agony it produces in the group. The experiment will quickly bring that problem to the surface.

The problem with determining prices by computation is that opportunities are often missed to charge greater than average margins or to penetrate important markets rapidly with low prices. Too often pricing arguments revolve around acceptable rather than creative and dramatic solutions.

Bob Davis, in his classic lectures on marketing, argues that many new products start out their lives as specialty items and evolve into commodities. The duty of marketing, he points out, is to keep refreshing the specialty nature of products. This differentiates products and, in turn, justifies price differentials.

Many high-tech products go through this evolution. In the case of semiconductors, products usually start out as single-source items and then evolve into commodities. For most semiconductor products, in time there will be at least three manufacturers worldwide producing functionally identical products. For "real" commodities, such as dynamic RAMS, there will at times be ten or more sources active in worldwide markets.

Other high-tech products never evolve into true commodities. In engineering workstations, a number of similar but not identical products are on the market. Many of them use the same operating systems. Some employ the same graphic standards. All are different, but those differences are becoming less important to many customers. In other words, the products are becoming "quasi-commodities."

The value of most high-tech products is determined by the cost of alternative solutions to the customer. In the case of the 80186, that customer could purchase fourteen other integrated circuits to solve the same problem.

But sometimes there is no alternative approach. Then, pricing is a matter of placing a value on the solution to a particular customer problem. That value has nothing to do with the cost of building the product.

As products become quasi-commodities, the value of the solution is increasingly determined by the price of comparable, though not identical, products. Here the price a customer is willing to pay is a function of the price of competitive offerings and of the value, both positive and negative, of the product's differences from the competitive offering. Here costs enter into the picture—but not so much those of the manufacturer itself, but of its competitors.

One of the greatest revelations to inexperienced marketing people is that *the market prices of quasi-commodities are not related to the costs in their own manufacturing area, but to the cost structure of the lower-cost competitors and their willingness to operate at certain margin levels.* Analyzing internal costs alone doesn't tell one very much about what can and will happen in the market. Internal costs only determine the willingness of a company to compete for business, not the price a customer is willing to pay.

Obviously, somebody's costs will set market prices. Usually that role belongs to the lowest-cost supplier. That is particularly true in a market with a number of competitors.

The traditional Japanese strategy has been to achieve the lowest costs possible and then to set market prices to achieve acceptable margins at those costs. (Of course, margins acceptable to a Japanese manufacturer would be suicidal to most of its non-Japanese competitors.)

Imagine there are two companies. One enjoys manufacturing costs 10 percent below the other's and is willing to operate at a 30 percent gross margin, while the competitor requires 40 percent. In this case, in order to meet its margin goals, the higher-cost supplier must establish prices 30 percent above those of its competitor. If the lower-cost manufacturer has a 20 percent manufacturing cost advantage and the same margin objectives apply, this translates into a 45 percent price advantage in the market for the lower-cost supplier (see Appendix B).

What all this means is that, for a company to compete effectively in a commodity market, it must be not only the lowest-cost manufacturer but also the lowest-overhead supplier.

DEVICE PRICING VERSUS PRODUCT PRICING

The value of any product to its market is strongly influenced by prices of competitive products. Many pricing errors are made because devices are analyzed, whereas products are priced.

When companies are engaged in comparing devices, they are not really involved in determining the value of the ultimate product to the market. The product features have dramatically different values, depending upon the market being served. And one feature that significantly influences the value of the product is its distribution channel.

A number of years ago Intel decided it had to offer power supplies to customers purchasing its single-board computer products. There appeared to be a large demand for such a product. Since the company did not have good power supply technology, Intel decided to purchase a device from a supplier and remarket it. Because of the markups that had to be applied to support Intel's costs and distributor margins, no real business for the product ever developed, but the power supply continued to sell in modest volume as a convenience item to users. Later, when Intel doubled the price, the sales volume remained the same. The value of easy availability through the distributor was apparently quite high to the casual user. On the other hand, the volume users, who had never been interested in the Intel product and had bought alternative solutions direct from other manufacturers to avoid distributor margins, had even less interest now. Thus distribution had great value to the convenience market segment and not much value to the volume user.

For certain market segments, services add significantly to the value of products. In some cases a product can't be sold unless a company is capable of providing adequate maintenance. Other customers, such as the federal government, require large amounts of specialized documentation and training. An entire service industry, known as the "Beltway Bandits," has grown up along the beltway around Washington, D.C., to offer that type of support to companies selling to the government.

Each significant difference in a product from its competitors generates a value gap. Much of the art of pricing a product depends on a determination of how much those differences are worth to a market segment. When a generic device is sold to many different market segments, the price of the item the customer buys is frequently differentiated through options. The generic device may remain inexpensive, but the options allow the company to raise its price so that it corresponds more closely to its value to the market segment.

Companies will be compensated for the true value of their products only if they first determine what those products are really worth to the market segment and then set prices accordingly. The best-run firms establish large price differentials based on large value differentials. That never happens when a company is selling products while cost analyzing devices.

CHARGE WHAT THE MARKET WILL BEAR, IF YOU DARE

The company that prices its unique products based on value to the customer is in essence charging what the market will bear. The theory is: If the value can be justified, the customers will pay it.

But charging "what the market will bear" usually carries a dramatically different connotation. For commodity-type products, this philosophy is usually associated with the establishment of prices in spot markets. Even though macho marketeers like to talk tough, few high-tech companies ever charge what the market will bear in that sense.

Whenever shortages develop in the semiconductor industry, a gray market develops. In 1983 many products were in short supply. The list price for an Intel 8031 was about $15, if you could get it. For our customers, shortages in those $15 parts were holding up the shipment of equipment costing thousands of dollars to manufacture. Here, if ever, was a real opportunity to price aggressively. The gray market price on the 8031 shot up to $150 before the bubble burst. But Intel never had the slightest inclination to raise prices above the $15 level.

Our reasoning was as follows: If the company takes advantage of a market perversion to make excessive profits, it will ultimately alienate and lose customers. Fifteen dollars was a fair price. It was a price the market could bear over the long term.

Some of Intel's customer's were not "afflicted" with the same morality. They argued forcefully for allocations that exceeded their actual needs, then sold the products at large markups in the gray market. That caused almost as much antagonism as if Intel itself had been guilty.

Customers have extremely long memories when they are unfairly treated, particularly when it comes to prices. Companies that charge what the market will bear in the short term should be prepared to live with the consequences later on, when the market again loosens up. Those firms will be the first to have orders canceled. Even more devastating, many customers quickly develop strategies to become independent of suppliers that price opportunistically. They take great pleasure in punishing past price gougers.

About the only high-tech suppliers who can truly take advantage of spot markets are brokerage firms. Those small companies have very low business momentum and can get in and out of markets quickly. Purchasing agents expect them to be opportunistic, because the broker's business is that of matching buyers and sellers. The broker is always dealing with customers at spot prices, sometimes well above the manufacturer's market price and at other times well below it.

Manufacturers, on the other hand, must take the long view. For them, charging what the market will bear and pricing on value are equivalent. If a supplier wants to hold its customer base, the price must be viewed as reasonable. You cannot take advantage of customers and still maintain their loyalty.

COMMODITIES USED TO BE
EASIER TO PRICE

Once, a gasket was a gasket was a gasket. All commodities were about the same in the customers' eyes.

Industrial purchasers are much smarter today than in the past. They have become keenly aware that they are purchasing more than the device. That in turn has led to the concept of buyer–seller co-destiny. Basically, co-destiny describes the realization on the part of both buyers and sellers that they can achieve a satisfactory relationship only if they admit their mutual dependence and act accordingly. The semiconductor industry provides many examples.

Big customers for semiconductors in recent years have been seeking reliable sources of supply to provide them with extremely high-quality parts. Customers have come to realize that the overhead cost of using a semiconductor in their product runs from 20 to 40 percent of the sale price of that product. They have also learned that the performance of their supplier greatly influences those costs.

The quality levels and failure rates of the chips are extremely important. If a company receives high-quality products from its supplier, it can dispense with incoming inspection, saving a considerable amount of direct cost and capital.

As the capital equipment to inspect complex integrated circuits now costs as much as a million dollars per system, obviously companies would love to avoid the purchase of a tester. But if a customer doesn't buy that equipment and hire the trained people to run it, it loses the ability to switch to unproven suppliers. Thus the customer becomes extremely dependent on the established sources of supply.

Customers have learned the value of predictable deliveries as well. With them they can escape large inventory investments and greatly reduce the purchasing staffs that monitor and expedite suppliers. But high levels of supplier performance can be achieved only if, in return, customers work with their suppliers to provide accurate forecasts and if suppliers tailor their manufacturing processes to customer cycles.

Co-destiny relationships become deeper with time. As customers become bigger and suppliers more concentrated, each side grows increasingly dependent on the other. Customers realize that if they want to have adequate capacity in place, they must plan its availability with suppliers. Large customers also have learned through bitter experience that having large numbers of suppliers for the same product does not assure supply, because most suppliers tend to run out of capacity at the same time. The only hope very large customers have for adequate supply is through mutual capacity planning with a limited number of suppliers.

As those relationships grow deeper, both suppliers and customers become increasingly dependent. The number of suppliers a customer deals with declines to a handful. In turn, other suppliers don't want to sell their precious capacity to these customers, because they know they will be dropped to support a key vendor in times of oversupply.

By the same token, suppliers also become more dependent. In order to meet the needs of their most important customers, they must often sacrifice other relationships. That means that some customers will grow wary of a supplier with deep commitments to other big customers. The less-favored customers will tend to go elsewhere, to vendors to whom they will be important.

In such co-destiny environments, strange things happen to pricing. Both sides suddenly become concerned about fairness. The poker game played at the purchasing agent's desk disappears, as the customer loses its ability to go elsewhere quickly and the supplier its flexibility to capture other customers.

When a $100-million-a-year customer decides to change suppliers, it is embarking on a very risky long-term project. It may never again find an adequate source. It also takes a supplier a long time to replace a $100-million-dollar customer. It may take only five or ten salespeople to service a very large account, but forty to fifty to capture that much new business. Just finding the qualified salespeople to develop new customers can take years.

In a co-destiny relationship, the customer becomes a unique market segment. The prices it pays will be below market in a boom and above market in a slump. If the customer is in a business where the prices of its products are continuously declining, the supplier will try to reduce prices steadily—even if there is no competitive pressure to do so. On the other hand, the customer that has reaped the benefits of capacity commitments in times of short supply must be willing to provide the seller with fair compensation when supply is abundant.

Pricing was a lot easier for commodity products before co-destiny emerged. In those days a supplier found out what a competitor was asking by reading the bid the purchasing agent left on his desk "by mistake" and then beating his competition by just the right amount. When a product was in short supply, it was fun to auction it off to the highest bidder. Gross margins in those days oscillated widely between 30 and 80 percent.

That era is all but over. In the future commodity suppliers will have to deal with the market price, the spot market price, and the co-destiny price. Of all those, the co-destiny price will be the hardest to determine. Both parties will try to exploit their positions in the relationship yet will know that a serious difference could be deadly.

PRICES AND MARKET POSITIONS

Prices and market positions are intimately related. The positioning of Timex will not support a premium-priced product. Similarly, low-priced Rolexes might sell well but would undermine the market for existing high-priced models.

In technology companies cost structures frequently evolve to support the price position of the company (or vice versa). Hewlett-Packard for years has been a premium-price supplier to the instrument market. Over time, customers have come to expect HP to produce very high-quality products with the latest features. They have also come to anticipate a high level of service and support from the company. That costs money, and customers have been conditioned to pay for it.

Intel is also a premium-price supplier. Customers expect superb products and a lot of technology support from the company. But the image has been detrimental to Intel when it has tried to enter high-volume commodity markets where price is a key issue. Here, some customers are so convinced the prices will be high that they never consider Intel as a potential supplier.

Those are problems created by customer perception. However, the image a company has of itself also does much to limit pricing flexibility. Companies become locked in on "acceptable" margins and have great difficulty accepting anything less. Sometimes the bias is so strong it leads companies to abandon businesses or makes it impossible for them to price their products competitively. If a company is used to commanding 55 percent gross margins, peer pressure within the company and direct management intervention are likely to bar any operations planning to price new products with, say, 40 percent margins, regardless of what the return on assets may be.

Companies should avoid participating in businesses where corporate positions inhibit them from pricing competitively. That, of course, is easy to say. But the fact is, where companies are intellectually incapable of accepting the price structure of a new business, the results are usually disastrous. Market share is often sacrificed to maintain margins—and, in short order, the company is driven out.

One might think it would be a relatively simple exercise to convince a company that dramatically different margins are acceptable for different product lines. Some companies actually do have such flexibility. But for others such a change is almost impossible until it is too late. Marketing people know the corporate position so well that they automatically develop pricing strategies compatible with it rather than with market needs. As a result the business is often unwittingly forfeited.

Before a product is developed for a market with a pricing structure incompatible with corporate goals, considerable special work must be done to ensure that the company will honestly accept the sacrifices it will have to make to be in the business. You'd better convince top management before you start.

DON'T FORGET DISTRIBUTION

When companies are faced with tough competitive situations, and as price pressures mount in the market, money must be saved to maintain profitability.

The easiest money to save is someone else's. Therefore, technology companies have consistently tried to lower product prices by providing slimmer margins to their distributors. Texas Instruments and Hewlett-Packard did so in the calculator business. Apple dealers grumbled that the company put them under excessive margin pressure.

But the classic case was Kaypro.

Kaypro, a supplier of transportable PCs, was notorious in the industry for providing low dealer margins. It was, of course, incapable of winning prime shelf space with those margins but was still able to move its products through second-tier retailers.

The weakest distributors, however, are the ones who need margins most especially in a shakeout period. That shakeout inevitably comes. Kaypro ultimately raised its margins somewhat, but it was too late. By then many of its distributors had been mortally wounded.

One of the rationales David Kay, Kaypro's vice president for marketing, used to justify the low margins was that since distributors would cut prices to compete with one another, Kaypro might as well keep the money for itself. Distributors do give away a lot of things, but not money when they are starving. When distributors give away margins it is usually because they feel forced into it by the competition. That happens most frequently in times of oversupply and when products are overdistributed. In Kaypro's case the retailers were being punished twice: first by low margins and then by overdistribution.

Pricing that does not provide sufficient margins for a distributor offers great opportunities for competitors. Pioneer, the Japanese manufacturer of audio equipment, used retail margins to gain an important position in the U.S. market. Pioneer merchandised its equipment at top-of-the-line prices but provided it to dealers at very low costs. Obviously, equipment with such high margins had very good sound and was of very high quality—or at least that's what dealers told their customers. Pioneer's real genius was in allowing dealers to discount to meet the prices of other competitors yet still make more margin on Pioneer's products. Pioneer ran over the market like a steamroller.

For some reason many technology companies believe their distributors are taking money they, the inventors, rightly deserve. Not surprisingly, then, lack of appreciation for distribution's contribution is always greatest among technology leaders. The followers in the market, anxious to steal the leader's market share, have much less trouble accepting the situation.

The fact is, distributors, dealers, and retailers do not make very large profits. The typical electronic industrial distributor makes about 5 percent pretax profit. It costs a lot to provide customers with acceptable service. Thus the margins paid to distributors for the most part are spent on customers.

Distribution is extremely expensive. For years companies and customers have tried to circumvent it. But, in spite of their efforts, distribution continues to grow. It does so because customers associate real value with the services distributors offer.

Technology companies find it difficult to believe that the mere handling of products, processing of orders, and maintenance of inventories can have such great value. After all, they reason, those mundane functions provide no leading-edge technology. But distributors know otherwise. For electronic component customers, the administrative and paper work savings associated with small-quantity orders often by themselves justify the use of distributors.

For all those reasons, customer pricing must take into account the needs of the distributor. It must provide adequate margins to assure the distributor fair compensation for the services it is rendering. Companies failing to provide for that will weaken an already weak distribution channel (for only the weak will tolerate that kind of action very long) or will find the distributor selling its services to another supplier—and there goes market share.

HIGH-TECH PRICING IS
VERY SUBJECTIVE

When a product becomes mature, it is easier to figure out what its price should be. By then market segments are better understood, and customer values are more precisely known. But even in very mature markets new pricing strategies constantly evolve to enable companies to tap new markets. One has only to look at the recent developments in the airline industry to appreciate the possibilities.

In the beginning, though, for many technology products all guideposts are missing. The products are new, the markets are new, and in many cases the customers are new. Even when the customer base is familiar, it is frequently going through such a rapid evolution that the value it attaches to particular products and services is perpetually changing.

In environments of great turmoil it is almost understandable why companies take the easy way out and compute what prices should be rather than try to determine how customers really value the product.

In consumer products, people seem to know what the price points are and have a keen understanding of how they relate to volume. But in all my years in technology marketing I have never seen a price–volume curve drawn that any marketeer would ever defend as more than a crude best guess. It's tough to be analytical when no one knows how price affects volume.

For many products it should be possible to determine value by adding up the costs of the items it is displacing. Presumably, if a customer can get the same for less or more for the same, he or she will take some technical risks. That strategy worked wonderfully for the Intel 80186. For $29.95, the customer could replace those fourteen other circuits at about the same cost. In the process the customers got higher performance, consumed less power, and saved printed-circuit board space. In such cases the displacement value is easy to compute. The benefits of the new product are easy to establish in the customer's mind.

But life is not always that easy.

Computer-aided engineering (CAE) equipment increases the productivity of engineers by some large amount that no one can really agree on. It reduces costly design errors. Most important, CAE significantly reduces design times, so products can get to market faster. For customers, the value of these products is so great that almost any price is too low. In fact, when CAE products were first introduced, price was limited only by the ability of suppliers to convince first-time customers of their worth.

Much of the agony was removed from the pricing process after the first CAE company chose its price. Then the price of the followers' products could be established relative to that first product. More capable products would presumably command a premium, and lesser machines with fewer features would sell for less. Of course, the reality isn't that simple, because there are many different CAE market segments. Some features are meaningful to certain customers and worthless to others. For example, Valid Logic's software runs on large mainframes. Customers desiring to integrate their CAE systems into corporate networks place a very high value on that capability. For engineers trying to avoid corporate control, on the other hand, the feature can be a handicap.

In such a market environment, the first substantial entrant gets to price on its product's absolute value to the customer. The followers then price their products based on their value relative to the first supplier's. As long as the market contains relatively few competitors, the products are likely to maintain this type of price relationship.

Of course, no business situation ever remains stable for long. Some competitor will inevitably break the rules and begin cutting prices. When that happens, the existing market order begins to collapse. Frequently one competitor, with or without a cost advantage, will attempt a preemptive strike. An all-out price war usually results.

According to the strategic principle discussed in Chapter 2, a company should have only one goal in setting prices: achieving a commanding position in the market segments it serves. But selecting a price to reach that goal is tricky. A low price may make it easier to sell the product initially, but impossible to support the customer or develop future products. As noted, the problem with the $360 price for the 8080 was not that customers wouldn't pay it but that it delayed future design decisions.

On the other hand, IBM's high prices were probably responsible for the creation of the computer business. The real problem customers faced when they bought data processing equipment was their own inability to put it to productive use. If computers could just be effectively applied, they would be priceless. High prices enabled IBM to help customers make their systems productive. That in turn built the market.

Rational pricing requires an understanding of the targeted segment, but companies frequently serve many segments. The problem therefore becomes one of developing pricing strategies to satisfy the needs of all segments. That is precisely what banks have done with their automated tellers, retail consumer services, and private banks. The price the customer pays for service is based on the size of his or her account with the bank. Depending on the magnitude of the account, the customer is served by an automated teller, a clerk, or a bank executive.

In the computer business it is the hardware and software options that enable a manufacturer to tailor the price to the market segment. The base price of a mainframe is usually set low enough so to appeal to a number of market segments. The pricing of the optional hardware and software is then structured in such a way as to value-price the system for distinct market segments.

Companies should understand what they hope to achieve before they set prices. As obvious as that may seem, it is frequently disregarded. The goal of a good pricing policy should be to attain a commanding position in the market segments a company is serving, not to compete in every market segment the product might conceivably fit. Products are frequently underpriced because companies try to satisfy the needs of too many different markets. Ironically, most incremental markets end up buying little anyway, because the product usually lacks many important features other than price. Of course, by then the opportunity to price the product for the majority of the customer base has been lost. More important, the sales force has wasted a lot of time calling on the wrong customers.

Good pricing sets prices at the highest possible level where the product still represents the best value for the market segments being served yet enables the company to achieve its market share goals. The pricing must be high enough to cover the cost of the product, distributor margins, the services a customer will demand, and provide a fair profit.

Once a company thinks it knows what the price of a product should be, that number should be tested. Prices for high-tech products are too frequently set internally with inadequate discussion between field sales, customers, and the marketing department. A salesperson must be able to convince a customer the price is fair. If the internal marketing organization can't sell the salesperson on the price, it is very doubtful the salesperson can in turn sell the customer.

For some reason salespeople are rarely presented with tightly reasoned arguments in justification of a product's value. Possibly that happens because it takes a lot of work to establish what the value of a product really is. Somebody has to figure out the cost of saving a worker-month of engineering time and has to establish what profits are lost if the customer can't get its product to the market on time. Not every salesperson has the time or the insight to do that work, nor should she. One job of a marketing group is to assimilate all the arguments generated by individual salespeople and to develop its own arguments, so that they can be used effectively throughout the company. By the way, the return on developing sound price arguments is quite high.

Customers, of course, have lots of opinions about price, and it is important to get their advice. Unfortunately, customers are usually unable to project accurately what they will be willing to pay until they have completely evaluated a product and have been exposed to all of its benefits. By then it may be too late.

A number of years ago I priced a product after doing an extensive survey of the customer base. Sales presentations were made to customers, and equipment was demonstrated. Price on one key option was presented as ranging from $695 to $1,195. Since the mainframe into which the options plugged was inexpensive, the prices of the options determined the price of the equipment. Customers could add as many as sixteen optional modules to the system.

From our discussion with the customers, it was obvious that they could easily justify the $695 price in their minds, but resistance started to develop above $800. Customers were appalled by the $1,195 figure. As our company earned good margins even at the lowest price, I finally settled on $795.

As we became more skilled in selling the product, it became obvious the customer could be persuaded to pay more. So the price was steadily raised, ultimately approaching the $1,195 we'd once lacked the courage to ask for. The fact was, no one had really known the value of the product. The customers were poor judges, because they had not been exposed to convincing arguments about the true value of the product. Until we got out and sold, we did not know how to convince the customer of its worth.

In the final analysis, pricing is extremely subjective. The price is right if it permits a company to earn fair profits and achieve its market share goals. But that still gives corporations quite a range. The price should be set at a point where—with practice—the value can be justified to the customer. The price can be very high, as long as the customer feels it is fair.

EIGHT

Be International or Fail

A LARGE PORTION of the market for most technology products is overseas. Many major U.S. corporations derive more than 30 percent of their income from international markets, and some up to 50 percent. At the same time foreign manufacturers (who in many cases have small local markets) have no choice but to export their products to remain viable. So, almost every manufacturer, whether it is in the United States, Europe, or Asia, should plan on being faced with foreign competition both at home and abroad.

Technology is no longer the exclusive province of a few advanced countries. It has become part of the national aspirations of both the mature and the developing countries of the world. The French government has targeted telecommunications, the Taiwanese and the Koreans are vitally interested in high-volume electronic parts, and the Japanese are interested in everything. Those and other countries have come to realize that as their standard of living rises, they will no longer be able to compete with the lower-cost labor areas of the world. The low labor content and high value-added nature of technology offers them a hope for the future. With its high intellectual content, technology businesses are the ideal battlefield on which advanced countries can wage their fight for economic survival.

The best international markets are those most similar to a com-

118

pany's home market. There, in many cases, one's product almost fits. There the job is easier. Unfortunately, few such markets exist.

In most cases a fair amount of work has to be done. The product may have to be modified. New types of distribution may be required. There may be a requirement (or a need) to manufacture in the local markets. The documentation may have to be translated. Even when considerable effort is needed, however, it is usually less than would be necessary to enter a new domestic market.

For some reason the compromises a company must make to succeed in a foreign market always seem excruciating. One reason is that such moves sometimes require a company to license its crown jewels, its technology. At other times a lot of hard work must be done that is not nearly as much fun as developing a new product. International markets require investments as well. The dollars spent in them are not available for other programs, the need for which may be more visible to local management. That hurts too.

On the other hand, the return on investment from international markets can be huge. Companies that refuse to participate in them not only lose important profit opportunities but will encourage foreign competitors to attack them at home. There are four principal reasons why an international market presence is essential.

REASON 1: LOST MARKET SHARE WILL HAUNT YOU

There was a time when the technology lead of the United States was so great that it had no competition. The industrial base of both Japan and Europe had been devastated by World War II. The United States owned the aircraft, electronics, semiconductor, and computer businesses—and many others as well. We could sell on our terms, and the market had to live by our rules.

That still goes on today in some market segments. If a company is marketing a breakthrough product, it will usually experience considerable initial export success. The overseas market will be so hungry for the new product that it will make compromises.

However, as the market matures, the customers will become more demanding. They will want to buy products that completely solve their problems, not ones that almost do. Then, if the company is going to continue to compete, it must adapt the product to local conditions.

Today most technology companies can no longer do business on

119

their own terms. If they do, they allow local suppliers to develop. They will soon be fighting them in other markets as well. A German, Korean, or Japanese manufacturer of dynamic RAMs can't remain satisfied with just its domestic market, which is too small. If it wants to get its costs down, it must export. The same is true in telecommunications systems, disc drives, printers, copiers, and cash registers.

In the final analysis, either you face an international competitor in its domestic market or in your own. So the game is to maximize worldwide market share. The domestic market becomes just another market segment. Conquer the world market, and you will have won the domestic one. But permit a foreign competitor to develop a substantial international market share, and you will soon have to fight an intense battle in your local market as well. Losing international market share almost always comes home to haunt you.

REASON 2: COMPETE TO STAY IN STEP

Once a company begins to participate in export markets, it is usually surprised by what it finds. In many cases foreign markets will be ahead of domestic ones, and there will be a chance to gain an insight into future trends. Observing from the outside is not enough. Only participation will give you the necessary wisdom.

If the U.S. steel and automotive industries had been active in the Japanese market (and I am not maintaining that the Japanese government would have allowed them to be), they would not have been taken by surprise by Japanese quality and cost structures. A similar myopia is apparent in U.S. high technology.

The U.S. semiconductor companies were caught off guard by the high level of Japanese quality. They were able to respond to it relatively quickly—at least quicker than the automotive companies—but nevertheless lost ground.

For a long time the U.S. manufacturers believed the Japanese were dumping products in foreign markets. In many cases they were, but that was too easy an excuse. After all, while the Japanese were "dumping" products, they were also building highly efficient production facilities. Their factories not only used less expensive labor, they were frequently more automated and more efficient. The Japanese in many cases also had better manufacturing strategies. U.S. companies active in the Japanese market picked up on that fact faster than the rest. Thus the international companies gained critical time to develop strategies to counter the threat.

I am not trying to argue the issues of protectionism, lower-cost capital, government support, less expensive labor, or other Japanese advantages. Those are simply facts about international competition. As long as they exist, a competitor must understand them and learn how to deal with them. Using the competitor's "unfair" advantages as an excuse to avoid the other lessons is not a valid defense, and certainly not an effective one.

The self-education process goes far beyond merely understanding the potential advantages and the structure of foreign competitors. New technology trends are developing in foreign markets. It is highly probable that the teletext, digital telephone networks, and videotext markets will develop more quickly in Europe and Japan than they will in the United States. If that happens, there will be a tremendous advantage to being there when it does.

The usual strategy of a country behind in a business sector is to protect its home market to permit indigenous suppliers to develop. The strong local suppliers who, with any luck, emerge are then encouraged to export their products. Industry leaders can minimize that competitive advantage by being on the scene the moment a country opens up and by making it as difficult as possible for local suppliers to gather momentum.

There is no better way to keep in touch than to be there. If you are succeeding in foreign markets, you will almost certainly be able to beat your overseas competitor in your own market. If you are failing in export markets, you'd better understand why. The reason for your failure overseas may become the same reason you will one day fail at home.

REASON 3: THE APPLICATION
BASE SHIFTS

Most TV sets purchased in the United States were once manufactured domestically. Now the majority are made overseas. Most cash registers now come from Japan. The same is true for VCRs and printers. A few years ago most of the subassemblies that went into small computers were made in the United States. Now a great proportion of them are subcontracted to low-cost assemblers in Asia.

If a company stakes its future on being the supplier to a domestic market and then the market moves away, that company is stuck. There's no great future in being the leading supplier to a dying industry. That is what happened to Rockwell in microprocessors: The calculator and cash register companies moved away.

The international market is very complex, and not all trends go in one direction. IBM and others are automating domestic facilities to keep production in the United States. Texas Instruments and Motorola are moving some of their assembly operations back from the Far East into automated facilities in the United States. Meanwhile, numerous high-tech firms continue to move manufacturing offshore.

It is not only component suppliers who have to worry about such trends. When new industries grow abroad, the markets for many products shift. Machine tool suppliers found that out, and so will U.S. manufacturers of CAE equipment. The engineers of Japan, Europe, Taiwan, and Korea are going to require automation too. The growth rate of the technical populations in many countries exceeds ours. If companies wish to lead in the world, they will have to follow the growth in the market.

I'd like to relate to you a truly perverse story about international markets to illustrate the point. For years American semiconductor companies have been singularly unenthusiastic about supplying components to the Pacific Basin, and with good reason. The prices there were the world's lowest, and those customers had the least loyalty to suppliers. To many, the Pacific Basin market was driven solely by price.

Of course, as more and more electronics manufacturers migrated to the Pacific Basin, supplier interest in that market increased. After all, who wanted to lose an established U.S. customer just because it shifted its manufacturing offshore?

But a funny thing happened when companies began to move their manufacturing overseas. Many went believing they could save a great deal on direct labor. What surprised most was that the cost of the direct material was substantially less as well. In fact, the savings on material was often several times greater than on the labor.

Well, who can blame a supplier for wanting to sell a part for four dollars instead of two? Or a customer for wanting to pay two dollars instead of four for the same product? The result was predictable: Customers set up purchasing operations in the Pacific Basin and imported the lower-cost material into the United States.

The irony of the situation was that the high domestic prices had in part been responsible for driving some of the customers overseas, just the place where the domestic suppliers did not want them to go.

Any time there are dislocations in a market, large price differentials may be created. Companies that can track the worldwide prices on a product can buy where it is to their advantage. If you are active in world markets, you can track the dislocations and respond.

Personally, I must admit that hard as I tried to predict the geographic trends in a given market, I was always surprised by what actually happened. Even though I felt I had become fairly knowledgeable, I was still regularly startled by the rapidity with which international trends developed. They moved so quickly that it was difficult for the sales channels to respond.

But, that said, I still hold that the lead time is longer if you are not in the international market at all. It is tough to keep up even when you do have a foreign presence, but almost impossible if you don't. A company must be present in all important markets for its products if it hopes to track shifts in the demand for its products in a timely fashion.

REASON 4: WORLD MARKETS ADD STABILITY

Despite the troubles companies have as a result of currency shifts, it is hard to make a convincing argument that world markets do anything but enhance corporate stability. For example, during one of the great U.S. semiconductor recessions, the Japanese market boomed. It was the only bright spot on Intel's corporate horizon.

Different markets often have different economic cycles. The traditional wisdom at Hewlett-Packard was that European economic cycles lagged behind those in the United States by six months. That always provided a nice cushion in both upturns and downturns.

But more is going on than just a phase-shift of economic cycles. The application bases in export markets are different as well. In Japan the consumer business for a long time dominated the economic fortunes of the electronics industry. Today in Europe the telecommunications and automotive electronics industries are becoming increasingly predominant. Those different application segments exert a stabilizing influence on the economic fortunes of a company, because they serve markets with different economic cycles.

Differences in economic cycles and application bases add stability. Companies with access to those markets gain an advantage.

INTERNATIONAL MARKETS
AND CORPORATE CONTROVERSY

I did business in international markets for almost twenty years, and I cannot remember a single trip where I didn't come home with a long list of things to be changed. A product might not meet the needs of the local market, or a commission plan not fit the local culture, or a service level not be right for the local customers—always something.

When I delivered my news, the rebuttal was almost always, "Why can't they do it our way?" I would reply that "they" could not because the market was different or "they" would not because they didn't have to or that "they" would simply be happier if we would accommodate them.

I wouldn't argue that such a xenophobic reaction is a uniquely American disease. Foreign companies fail for the same reason. We all feel more comfortable with what we know, and we have a hard time understanding why what seems reasonable to us does not look the same to a person in another country.

The most obvious and understandable problems in this regard relate to product specifications. The Germans want their electrical equipment to meet VDE (equivalent to Underwriters Laboratory) electrical specifications. It is a reasonable request. The Europeans have different communications standards as well. And they want components to conform. If they don't, you can't sell them in those markets.

Differences of that kind are easy to accept. Others are more difficult. Take service. The Japanese demand all sorts of services from their suppliers. I'm personally convinced that many Japanese companies think of suppliers as servants. This attitude tends to make Americans bristle.

For many years Intel had been a significant supplier to the Japanese market. One of its customers, Fanuc, today the world's leading supplier of machine tool controls, was having a quality problem with the 8086. The parts had gone through incoming inspection without difficulty, but one out of every five hundred or so failed at the final system test. Now, Intel had shipped hundreds of thousands of the parts, and no one else had ever complained. But Fanuc demanded answers.

To understand why the matter was so important to Fanuc, one has to understand a little bit about that company. It has a world reputation for quality. When I visited the company, I had been amazed at what I had seen. Fanuc had posted a mean-time-to-failure objective on the order of five years. By comparison, most of their competitors dreamed in terms of months between failures. A few months prior to my trip, Intel had been visited by a domestic supplier who was having problems in the market because Fanuc's products were ten times more reliable. In short, Fanuc's quality systems were superb.

Fanuc wanted to know why each of the fifty or so Intel parts had failed. That level of analysis was very time-consuming and demanded a very talented person. In fact, the analysis ultimately cost Intel more than $20,000. When the customer has spent less than a half a million dollars for parts, that's a lot of failure analysis.

Eventually Intel discovered that the test programs it used to screen its parts did not cover all modes of failures. Fanuc was not surprised. It claimed to have had the same problem with other suppliers. It was, however, extremely angry about the length of time Intel took to find the answer. To Fanuc, its request had been more than reasonable—and by local standards it was. To Intel, however, it was almost irrational and a very great inconvenience. After all, every other customer was happy.

Ultimately Intel's solution to providing the proper service to the Japanese market was to invest in a local failure analysis facility. As the test equipment required to do the job cost hundreds of thousands of dollars, that was an expensive proposition. But it also was the only way to guarantee service to that market, and it put an end to subsequent controversy over that type of service.

There are many other examples of expensive compromises domestic companies have had to make to become acceptable vendors to foreign customers. European customers want locally manufactured products. Many are under governmental pressure to increase their local content, so they are extremely anxious to buy devices made in the Common Market. But local manufacture can raise the cost of supplying a product and ultimately the price to the customer. Still, companies are forced by government pressure to demand it. Local manufacture is a lot of extra work for manufacturing groups, and frequently they will fight it. But sometimes it must be done.

Time differences add further stress. Europeans are always in bed or out to dinner when you want to talk with them; likewise the Japanese. The narrow communication windows are further aggravated by transit delays, which cause people endlessly, and infuriatingly, to interrupt one another during phone conversations. Add the language problems, and you are setting the stage for regular misunderstandings.

International markets, in short, are an inconvenience to most companies. They are always requiring changes in the product, policy, and service and are perpetually plagued with communication problems. Because they are a drain on corporate resources and inhibit companies from inventing their next product, going international is frequently a source of conflict. Companies must therefore continually be sold on the value of international participation.

That, of course, is marketing's job.

THE PRODUCT IS ALMOST RIGHT

The vast majority of products sold in international markets are almost right.

Almost every foreign country is a different market segment. Depending on the laws and culture of the country, the barriers to market entry can range from large to trivial. The political, cultural, and technical barriers are quite high in entering the Japanese market, making that market more difficult to penetrate than most.

But here again, we must return to the key point that the product is far more than the device.

Sometimes the device is right for a market, but the product is not. For example, the sales presentation that works in one country may not play at all in another. If one country has engineers in short supply, it is probably very interested in increasing the productivity of the ones it has. That is an effective argument for selling CAE and development system equipment. In the Pacific Basin, in contrast, the perceived value for that type of equipment is much less because of the plenitude of lower-priced talent.

As I have noted, the level of quality customers demand may differ considerably. The level of sales service required is usually different as well. In U.S. and European markets, large customers are happy to deal with both manufacturers and distributors. They simply award their large purchase orders to manufacturers and the smaller ones to the distributors. They do so for good reason: The distributor is structured to handle low-volume business efficiently and to give quick response from its local inventory, but its prices are too high on the big deals.

In Japan business is not done that way. It is either all direct with the manufacturer or all through distribution. When large companies place low-quantity orders, they expect the same fast and efficient service from the manufacturer that they'd get from a distributor.

Most system products must be tailored to local markets. The most obvious special needs include sales material, manuals, and customer training courses, all usually in a different language. The electrical requirements of many countries are also different. Most companies handle the voltage and power problems well but are caught off guard by the various safety requirements. Europeans also have special standards for computer terminals to reduce the stress on office workers. They are not hard to meet, but a company must be aware of them first.

Requirements for application programs can vary widely as well. Required changes range from minor modifications to accounting programs to total system redesign. A good example of the last are the efforts of companies to attack text processing in Japanese and Chinese.

Of course, there is no such thing as the universal promotion. I almost never liked the British Intel ads. They in turn thought our material was awful. The British, for some strange reason, were never fond of references to the nickel cigar and George Washington. But the differences went deeper. There are no pan-European publications for most markets, so trade shows take on much greater importance than they do for U.S. customers.

The competitive picture varies dramatically from country to country. In semiconductors, Siemens was a very effective competitor for Intel in Germany, Scandinavia, and Italy but had weaker distribution in other European countries and was not a factor at all in the Japanese and U.S. markets. The French are attempting to protect their indigenous semiconductor suppliers, which results in less Japanese competition there.

In almost every country the strength of key competitors will vary. That is partly a function of their willingness to adapt their product to the market, but more commonly it depends on their ability to build adequate distribution there. Be that as it may, who your competitor is determines what your product must be.

In every foreign market the complete product varies. The companies that are most effective are the ones willing to shape their product to the market place.

THE COST OF NATIONALISM

The foreign supplier can expect to incur a cost associated with nationalism. There was a time when prices in foreign markets were often higher than in the United States. That happens less frequently today. Ten years ago it was easy for technology companies to pass on the added costs of doing business in foreign markets. Customers understood they had to pay the surcharges to cover the added costs of doing business—duty, freight, and currency exchange. They had little choice.

Today the manufacture of technology products is scattered throughout the world. Now there are local suppliers, foreign suppliers with local manufacturing, and exporters to deal with. These days there is a local market price, not a foreign price with local surcharges. If there is a manufacturer in Germany, its costs are not greatly affected by fluctuations in the deutschemark. If the mark weakens against the dollar and the yen, the German firm does not have to raise its prices to compensate. A U.S. or Japanese supplier without local German manufacturing either has to meet that price and lose profits or give up market share.

There is little doubt that most companies experience added costs from doing business in foreign markets. A tremendous amount of additional administrative work must be done. Small local factories usually cost more to operate and are less efficient than large, centralized ones. The costs of local promotion are quite high.

That's just the beginning. A company sometimes must make enormous expenditures to support the national goals of the countries in which they are doing business. For example, in order to develop local markets for semiconductors, local second sources are frequently required by customers or by "law." That means semiconductor companies must actually license competitors to build their products. There actually are a few benefits to doing so, most frequently added market share. However, it also creates a new competitor. Most companies don't need that kind of help. This happens in all kinds of manufacturing, not just semiconductors. Joint ventures have become a way of life for companies hoping to develop local markets in the Pacific Basin. Corning has a joint venture with Samsung to make TV picture tubes in Korea. Hewlett-Packard has a joint venture with Yokagawa Electric Works in Japan and Samsung in Korea. Tokyo Electron and Thermco have formed a company to supply diffusion furnaces to the Japanese market. It would be nice to be able to keep the business to oneself, but frequently the only choices are either to cooperate or to surrender the market.

To summarize, once a company becomes an important supplier to a local market, it is almost always pressured to pay tribute to nationalism. The key is to figure out ways to benefit from the situation.

CURRENCY FLUCTUATIONS AND MARKET SHARE

We live in a world of volatile currencies. One minute the French franc is four to the dollar and the next it is ten. The Japanese market, with all its nationalistic barriers, is tough enough to penetrate, but when the yen weakens against the dollar by 10 percent it can wipe out the slim profits most companies exporting to that market manage to scrape out.

There is a tendency among most companies to become interested in exporting when domestic currencies are weak and then to withdraw from those same markets when currencies are strong. Even, if a company doesn't fully withdraw, it frequently gives up big chunks of market share by raising prices in an ill-advised attempt to sustain margins.

Once market share is lost it is extremely difficult to regain. When a company is in a high-growth business, it is just about impossible to regain one's position. If, on top of that, a company lets its sales and distribution channels deteriorate because of currency fluctuations, it is all but finished.

It would be foolish to maintain that a company should go for market share with complete lack of regard for profitability and the effect currency fluctuations have upon it. Rather, its efforts should be directed toward isolating itself as much as possible from their destructive effects. Perhaps the strongest argument for local manufacturing is that it tends to protect companies from currency fluctuations.

Companies that plan to build important positions in foreign markets must have long-term strategies. Those strategies should be as invulnerable as possible to currency fluctuations. A company can't turn on an assault on the market one minute and turn it off the next and hope to succeed.

INTERNATIONAL ORGANIZATIONS
SHOULD BE HIGH-LEVEL

A company hoping to be a significant player in a foreign market is going to be faced with some very tough decisions. New products must be developed. Factories may have to be built. Joint ventures might have to be formed. Technology exchanges may have to be negotiated. Pricing authority will probably have to be delegated.

Many foreign operations start off as overgrown sales channels. They acquire marketing capability and then evolve into profit-and-loss centers. Thus they are often staffed with lesser talents. That is unfortunate, for the job of running foreign operations is extremely complex. In fact, it is a more difficult job than most general management positions.

Consider the work. Personnel are widely dispersed. Each country has a different set of laws with which the company must comply. In many cases international managers find themselves dealing directly with presidents of large corporations and high-level government officials. Opportunities to embarrass the company abound.

A few years ago I got a lesson in foreign intrigue that still embarrasses me today. The French government approached Intel about entering into a joint venture with a domestic company. Most of Intel management was dead-set against the proposals, but Bob Noyce and I were for it, and, at an emotional session, we prevailed.

It was my argument that carried the day. I made an extremely simple case. It was that there had to be some price at which Intel might want to deal. We all then agreed that $10 million was the right number. I realized later that the figure was acceptable to the other Intel executives because they were all convinced we could never get it.

So Jerry Diamond, a very skilled negotiator with lots of international experience; Bernard Giroud, the French country manager; and I went after the order. Bob Noyce gave lots of help.

The strategy we pursued was fairly direct. We asked for $25 million, thinking we would then retreat down to an acceptable level. Instead, remarkably, they accepted. We returned, ecstatic, with an agreement in principle.

Then, just about the time we should have been signing the deal, the French changed the corporate partner to someone I felt would not be acceptable to Intel. In order to stall for time while Intel could ponder the merits of the new partner, Jerry and I raised the price to $50 million. We told the French we thought we could get corporate approval at the higher price. To our amazement, the French agreed to the new price. The deal was approved by the Prime Minister.

The French were happy. I was happy. But Intel was increasingly dismayed as it learned more about the new partner. Ultimately, the company decided to kill the deal.

Now the rule at Intel is that the person who starts a job gets to finish it. Jerry and I, with our tails between our legs, flew back to France to meet with a high-ranking government official who was also flying back to Paris to join us. The difference was we were flying tourist and bringing bad news, and he was returning on the Concorde to celebrate the deal with us at Taillevent, a three-star Parisian restaurant.

I never realized how much indigestion a rich French meal could cause. The French were, of course, wrong for changing the partner, but I was wrong as well in not breaking off negotiations right then. But I believed I could sell the company on a deal I thought was good for both parties.

It took years for Intel to rebuild its relationship with the French government after that. ''Luckily'' Mitterand was elected President, high-level officials were replaced, and the new Prime Minister didn't know our name.

Neither the French nor Intel had intended to act in bad faith, but by the time we were through, each of us suspected the other. Probably a more experienced person would have avoided the trap. On the other hand, everyone at Intel thought I was fairly experienced—and look how I messed it up.

Being successful in international markets requires companies to make important decisions. But on top of that it requires that companies make compromises. The corporate culture must be shaped to the local market. Credit policies may have to be changed. A lot of important little decisions must be delegated to local management. Low-level management just can't be left to do that job.

The most significant management problems in international operations usually develop when responsibility has been delegated to too low a level in the home office. The typical scenario is one where individuals who don't understand the market attempt to manage it at the detail level. They try to call the shots on pricing and promotions based on their knowledge of the domestic market. Worst of all, they try to force foreign operations into conformity with ''the way it is done in the home market.''

In truth, details are precisely the wrong things to manage. The organization quickly goes into paralysis as it tries to deal with impossible challenges in pricing, credit, and promotions. In short order, while internal debate rages, competitors begin to steal orders. A tremendous amount of energy is spent on simple issues while the complex and important ones are forgotten. As pennies are debated, corporate birthrights are given away.

The development of foreign markets requires experienced hands. If you can't trust the management of your company's foreign operation, then change it—now.

ATTACK ABROAD

If your company is a leader, the place to fight the battle for the international market is abroad. By being a strong supplier to all markets, a company can sometimes preempt the need for local suppliers. Even if strong local competitors do develop, their success can be made less likely. The weaker a competitor can be kept in its home market, the less likely it is to encroach on markets elsewhere.

The strategy of a follower, on the other hand, is to develop domestic markets first. For one thing, it is easier to succeed there. Customers are more tolerant and more amenable to giving a local supplier the edge. Sometimes even the government will help. That, of course, has been the Japanese strategy, but it is used by other countries as well. It's how Brazil got into the aircraft business and how European semiconductor companies are attempting to regain their strength.

Fighting the battle abroad takes strong, senior people. The decisions to be made are both big and important. You cannot make them at home. It is very difficult to make intelligent decisions on how to respond to local market conditions and how to fix anything when you are ten time zones and 6,000 miles away from the problem. If you want the local management to be effective, be prepared to delegate decision-making to it.

NINE

Plan Products, Not Devices

S UCCESS IS A FUNCTION of doing the right things well. If you can do that without a plan, then you don't need to spend time documenting strategies and tactics and constantly looking at view-graphs. Instead, you can be out doing.

Unfortunately, most of us can't execute effectively without following some type of plan. We need it.

The most serious mistakes companies make are usually the result of poor planning. By the time a company finds itself going after the wrong market, with the wrong product, at the wrong time, it is usually in such a tight box that only Houdini could get it out.

In the really big high-tech markets, companies can find themselves faced with as many as fifty competitors. That was the problem companies in the minicomputer, personal computer, digital watch, and electronic calculator markets faced. In most cases only three or four survived. (One wonders if the losers' plans had been prefaced with the realistic admonition that a new company would require a $50 million investment and that there was a 5 percent chance of success *if* any of them would have been funded.)

Errors in execution can also be catastrophic, but there is usually more hope of correcting them. If a company is in the right place at the right time with the right product, a lot of mistakes can be fixed. Of course, momentum is lost, but this may not be fatal.

Few business plans, unfortunately, incorporate the "Strategic Principle." That's why most new companies fail. Of course, a plan made in accordance with the principle is not guaranteed success, but the odds are certainly better.

CAN YOU REALLY PLAN A HIGH-TECH PRODUCT?

The essence of high-tech is doing new things for new markets. Companies can't look around, see what others have done, and model their plans after them. The models don't exist. Nor can you analyze the weaknesses of a competitor that isn't there. You can only speculate about potentialities and argue over contingencies.

One problem faced by high-tech companies in recent years arises from the overabundance of easily available venture capital. A company can have a great idea and enthusiastically pursue its implementation, only to find out that ten other companies have also been founded to attack the same market. It is very difficult to make any plans in such an environment.

In the end, most plans can only spell out the general direction a company should take and where it should end up. Plans almost never address all the major problems the company will face. Even the best plans usually contain near-fatal flaws that must be corrected during implementation. A good example is a perfect plan we developed for an 8-bit microcontroller at Intel.

Formal product planning really started at Intel when Les Vadasz organized the "MCS (Microcomputer system) for Lunch Bunch." The Lunch Bunch met once a week, and one of its first projects was to plan the successor to the 4004, the world's first microcomputer. At the time we knew, or thought we did, a lot about the microcomputer market. We knew the 4-bit 4004 was too slow and that we could build an 8-bit system for almost the same cost. We also knew we needed a system substantially faster and with more memory.

We understood a lot of other subtle things about the market as well. For example, we recognized the problems customers were having getting their initial designs to work. For that reason, we planned a special version of the part customers could use for prototyping.

After a number of meetings the 8048 was born. We had planned the perfect product, and we knew it. What was more, the 8048 was going to make use of a number of Intel proprietary technologies, which our competitors would have great difficulty duplicating. As we described the product to customers, their enthusiasm grew. We knew we had a winner on our hands.

As discussed earlier, our euphoria did not last long. The balloon was burst by the Fairchild 3870. No one with knowledge of the semiconductor industry would ever in their wildest dreams have anticipated an attack from that quarter. Once great, Fairchild had been fading for years. The firm had never been a factor in the microcomputer market, and there was little reason to expect it ever would be. Fairchild also had lost most of its good people. It was therefore all but inconceivable that a second-string squad from a last-place team could be doing that to us.

But they were, and we were losing orders all over the place. Our perfect product was not so perfect after all.

We learned later that Fairchild had hired some talented people with consumer electronics backgrounds. They knew what the high-volume accounts—designing telephones and automobiles—wanted. The 8048 had been planned for the traditional Intel customer base, which manufactured more sophisticated systems in lower volumes. As a consequence, the 8048 had many features that were of little value to the high-volume customers and lacked some they really wanted.

In the emotionally charged world of high-tech, elation can turn to depression overnight. For Intel, things went from bad to worse as Fairchild signed up Motorola and Mostek as second sources. That gave Fairchild creditable support in the market place and provided capacity to build the 3870 in the necessary volumes.

Before long the Fairchild 3870 was being quoted in the market at well below Intel's manufacturing cost. The Intel field organization was going crazy over its inability to compete. I visited one customer designing telephones in Chicago and left shaking my head as a 250,000-unit order evaporated before my eyes. Similar horror stories came in from around the country. Our perfect product had turned into a real dog.

We had to do something. Intel went into a strategic rethink. In the end we decided to give up on the big deals and direct our efforts to the customer base for whom we had planned the product in the first place. Strange as it may seem, in business it is very easy to forget what you set out to do. In the heat of battle you become so concerned about an opponent, you decide to attack him on his ground rather than stand on your own.

Before long Intel was winning deals again, not in the volume applications, but in the smaller ones, where the customers needed all the support, features, and services we could offer.

Something else happened as well. The market tightened up for all semicondutor devices. Customers couldn't get the 3870 in the quantities they wanted. Soon our opponents were "welching" on the big low-price deals. Within a few years the 3870 was no longer a factor in the market place. Meanwhile the 8048, by being available in sufficient quantities, had become the dominant product. Intel had at last achieved the position it once thought its due.

How do you plan for such an eventuality? You can't. A good plan can only increase your chances of success. But never, ever trust the plan completely. Results depend on implementation. The job is only 10 percent done when the plan is complete. Nevertheless, good plans can help a company avoid many pitfalls and can increase its chances of success. Great plans do not build a great company, but they are certainly part of the foundation.

IN HIGH-TECH THE CUSTOMER
OFTEN COMES LAST

The customer should always be first, but much of the time in high-tech the customer comes last.

What usually happens is that an engineer in the laboratory thinks up something new. Everyone gets enthusiastic about the idea, and a project is born. As the program matures, marketing finally gets involved in finding customers who need the device.

Obviously this is not a particularly customer-oriented approach. Most young MBAs would be offended by the process. But that's how things often happen. Customers did not ask Intel to build the EPROM. In fact, even after the product existed, customers couldn't tell us exactly how they were going to use it. Most figured it would be applied only in low volumes, because the price was not competitive with ROMs (read only memories). But EPROMs turned out so convenient to use compared with ROMs that they ultimately ended up more popular than anyone imagined.

It took competitors a long time to figure out that EPROMs appealed to a large market, not a specialty one. Our marketing counterparts at other firms missed the opportunity because, like us, they assumed no volume market would ever develop. Score one for the technologists.

Well, you may agree, the market for EPROMs is pretty arcane. Surely for something more self-evident, like the microprocessor, the potential would have been obvious. After all, didn't the "computer on a chip" start the second industrial revolution?

Well, I can tell you that wasn't the case at all.

As Ted Hoff, the inventor of the microprocessor, was listening to a Japanese customer one day, it occurred to him that the customer was trying to solve his problem in the wrong way. As a result of the discussion, Ted conceived of the microprocessor. An Intel engineer had just discovered one of the great inventions of the century. What an opportunity!

Of course, you can guess what happened next. Marketing decided there was a very small market for such a product and dragged its feet. Finally, engineering announced it was fed up and was going to introduce the product itself if marketing wouldn't get on the ball.

Intel wasn't alone. Rockwell, which had a microprocessor soon after Intel, and a superior one at that, eschewed the general-purpose market, altogether convinced that a serious business couldn't be developed.

Anyone who has been around high-tech for a long time will have a collection of these stories. I have probably talked to a half-dozen companies that turned down the original Haloid patents, the basis for Xerox machines, because carbon copies and mimeographing were so much cheaper. GE had the first transistorized computer but did not sell it on the open market, because company management was convinced that the computer was a special-purpose device useful only for banks.

Indeed, marketing's record is pretty lousy when it comes to exploiting new technologies. When technologies become more mature and the problem becomes one of extension and refinement, however, the quality of marketing input grows measurably. By then customers have much better insight into what they want. They've lived with the product for a while and used it to solve problems. Usually they've developed a list of needs and requirements, some of which would never have occurred to the development group.

MARKET SEGMENTS DEMAND
COMPLETE PRODUCTS

To my way of thinking, the first task in planning is identifying the target market segment. Not the broad horizontal market, but the market where the company is going to sell its products.

It does little good for a company to quote data about the $50 billion computer market and then announce a plan to sell just $20 million worth of equipment to that market. If a company plans to be a successful small fish in a big pond, it will succeed only if it holds a commanding position in a smaller submarket.

Most executives have grown sick of seeing endless tables of market data from various studies by independent research firms. And with good reason. Such data provide answers to only the most general questions and rarely provide the kind of specific insight necessary for strategic or operational decisions. For example, at Intel research by Dataquest was often used as a source of information about the semiconductor and computer markets. For the most part the information was very accurate, and it gave a good sense of the general direction in which those markets were heading. But beyond that the information was not valuable. Using it was like trying to navigate with a compass: You can tell the direction in which you are headed, but not where you are or how to get where you want to go.

The principal planning mistake companies make is to fail to define with great precision the market they intend to attack. If you can't define who the customer is, how can you invent a product that will satisfy its needs? Further, if you can't articulate the entry barriers to the targeted market segment, it will be impossible to develop even a gross estimate of what the cost of market entry will be.

Perhaps the best example I know of not fully understanding a market has occurred in the "fail-safe" computer business. Because of redundant circuitry, fail-safe computers supposedly never stop. They are used in critical applications where a computer failure can cause severe losses to a customer, as in airline reservations, automated bank tellers, and air traffic control. The leading company in the business is Tandem Computer.

I served on the Board of Directors of Tandem when the company started. At the time, there was a tremendous interest in fail-safe systems. The company quickly learned that while the fail-safe attribute was an attractive feature, it was only one of many reasons why

138

customers wanted Tandem's computer. Ease of expandability, for example, seemed to be even more important.

I recently had lunch with Jim Treybig, Tandem's president, and asked him to characterize the unique strengths of his company. Jim had a long list, but the item that stood out in my mind was his statement that Tandem was the only company in the world that could supply a customer with a worldwide network that could effectively support 10,000 people using the system all at once. That application required the unique communications and data base software that ran on the Tandem computer. The fail-safe feature turned out to be just the icing on the cake.

Tandem has had its problems, but it has also grown into a profitable $600 million company in less than fifteen years. In the process it has attracted a lot of competition. Because of my prior involvement with the company, I have been asked in recent years to review a lot of business plans of would-be competitors. Not one of those entrepreneurs was ever able to articulate the market segment he was pursuing.

Developing the basic hardware and software for a computer system represents about one-half the cost of the finished product. So here, in the fail-safe computer business, were companies that understood only what half their final development cost was going to be. Even more important, much of the work those companies were doing could not be effectively tailored to the market segment, because that segment's characteristics weren't fully comprehended.

Fail-safe computer companies aren't the only ones with this problem. CAE companies certainly have it. And the same disease has afflicted the microcomputer system business from the beginning.

I have read lots of business plans in my day. Nine out of ten have failed in precisely and succinctly defining the target market segment.

Complete products are the key to a company's success, and it is impossible to determine what a complete product is unless a company understands its market segment. In immature businesses, nearly every company is in the process of product completion. There is an unending list of demands coming from within and outside the company for more features, better promotions, and new distribution channels. The length of the list and the urgency of the requests are determined by both the customers and the competition.

When companies have not properly planned for the market segment, the list becomes quite long. If a company attacks too many market segments at once, the list becomes even longer and at times self-contradictory. When that happens, the product will never be completed.

Most new market entrants attack too broad a market. Then, when they encounter adversity, such firms tend to retreat—either consciously or unconsciously—to a more proper, more narrowly defined market segment. But in the meantime they have wasted precious time and resources. They have added features to their products to make them more appealing to markets they have now abandoned. Had those same resources initially been spent on the ultimate narrow market segments, those firms would have had a much stronger position and a far greater chance of survival.

It is far better to establish a strong beachhead and expand than to have to retreat to a defensible position with the enemy in hot pursuit.

PLAN FOR COMMANDING POSITIONS

I once listened to a very slick presentation by a marketing manager at Hewlett-Packard. He wanted to pursue the commercial computer market and assured management that his plan was sure to succeed. His rationale was that he needed only a 2 percent market share in order to meet the goal. The man had a plan for disaster, not for success. Of course, HP management realized this.

A company should always plan to achieve commanding positions. If its goal is to achieve $100 million in sales in five years, then the company should aim at $100 million to $400 million market segments. A company must make it a goal to capture at least 25 percent of a market segment. It should never even enter a market unless it is almost certain it can capture at least 15 percent.

For very big markets, most companies never have a hope of achieving such a goal. The only chance a small company has in a very big market is if it gets there first or is blessed with some kind of breakthrough. That is precisely what happened to Apple and Intel. They seized the lead before the giants even decided they wanted to join the race. It was not true for IBM-compatible PC manufacturers. Instead, they were late entrants to an investment-intensive business. Today the only ones left are those that differentiated themselves and claimed market niches.

It is very difficult to purchase information about the size of a market segment. There are several reasons. The first is that only a few companies are really interested in data on any given niche—not enough to pay for the research by an independent firm. The second is that there are almost an infinite number of ways to slice up any market. It is the marketing department's job to figure out ways to carve up a market to its advantage, and they are usually not along the lines that would satisfy a market research firm. Therefore, it is unlikely that the available data about market segments really will either exist or apply to a particular corporate strategy. In fact, if such data are already available you probably should reconsider your plan. After all, if you can read about a market segment in a study, the market is probably too mature to contemplate entering.

If a company knows the size of a total market, it can probably estimate the size of its market segment within a factor of two. I know that sounds very imprecise, but with a new technology it's about as close as you are going to get. So be wary of precise market data.

In the end, gross estimates are better than none. Marketing groups should be forced to continue their planning exercises until they can define a market segment whose size is compatible with the company's business objectives.

Beyond that, the group should be forced to define why its choice is truly a market segment of importance. It is not enough to merely select "the computer market for medical institutions" if a company can't define the barriers to market entry. A company should try to determine what the cost of vaulting those barriers will be not only for itself but for competitors.

Barriers vary—both the ones the company will encounter and the ones it will erect, such as patents. Unique distribution channels are very difficult to duplicate, as are customer support structures. Companies should contemplate just what the barriers are and their size relative to the market segment. If the barriers are large in relation to the size of the segment, there is a good chance a company positioned within will not be attacked by competitors. Even if it is, there is a high probability the attack will fail.

For most companies, planning for a commanding market segment position is at best an imprecise exercise. Nevertheless, it is a useful one. By engaging in the analysis, a company will narrow its focus and avoid catastrophic mistakes. In this way, even if a company can't realistically plan to capture 50 percent of a market, at least it won't settle for just 2 percent.

If a plan does not articulate a market well enough to define a commanding position, maybe it is not a plan at all.

WHAT IS A MARKETING PLAN?

A marketing plan is the basic document embodying marketing invention. It should clearly identify the market segment of interest and should contain necessary information about the segment's size and the customer population. The plan should also articulate the barriers to market entry relative to that segment and should estimate the costs of crossing those barriers.

Admittedly, all that cannot be done with great precision, but rough estimates are better than none at all. Most new business plans are not run aground by estimates that are off by 30 percent. Management can deal with that kind of error. It cannot cope with market predictions off by a factor of three or more or when the cost of market development is off by a factor of two. These are irrecoverable (and usually unconscionable) planning errors.

A good marketing plan should also contain an analysis of important competitors—not all of them, but the ones that count. The focus should be on the activity of those competitors in market segments of interest. Sometimes competitors appear to be very formidable from a distance but very vulnerable up close. Looked at as a whole, there is frequently no way a small company can see how to beat a large, monolithic one. But when the activities of large companies within smaller market segments are analyzed, exploitable weaknesses begin to appear.

Once the competition and the market segments are understood, a marketing plan should define market share goals, that is, they should commit the company to attaining a commanding position.

If a company is incapable of developing a rational plan for attaining those goals, it is unlikely ever to reach them in practice. Companies unable to plan for commanding marketing positions should get new product marketing managers, select a different market segment, or kill the program. You plan for success or you don't plan at all.

The next step is to invent a great product. Assuming that the device's characteristics reasonably match customers' needs, the marketing plan should spell out how the product will be differentiated, positioned, promoted, distributed, priced, supported, and serviced.

Finally, marketing plans should contain schedules and budgets. You need the spreadsheets.

Marketing plans are frequently long, often more than two hundred pages. Most of those pages are destined to be unread. I'm convinced the only people who know what is in a plan of that length are the people who wrote it in the first place. A marketing plan should be a communication document. If it is of epic length, a plan is not communicative. I have always found the best approach to market planning is to keep the plans short, summarized on twenty or so transparencies.

Marketing plans for technology businesses should be living documents. Because technology businesses change quickly, most plans are obsolete within ninety days. Who has time to redo a 200-page plan every three months? Regular review is thus a most valuable part of the planning process. It forces the firm to reexamine competition on a regular basis.

The plan review is also an excellent tool for communicating with the advertising agency. Once the ad agency understands the company's marketing plan, the quality of its output should improve. Each review forces a company to ask itself what has changed about the market segment it is serving and how it must adapt the product to the customer base. It also forces the firm to track its progress toward its stated goals.

Review sessions should not be management inquisitions, but problem-solving sessions where the best marketing minds involved on the project try to improve their understanding of market conditions and to determine the company's future strategy.

Marketing plans should be not monuments but living documents that provide direction to every individual involved in marketing the product. They are, as well, the conceptual tools that embody marketing invention. Marketing plans are the heart of new product development.

THREE TYPES OF PLANS

In my experience companies create three types of plans: device, product, and business plans.

In a device plan the company plans only the characteristics of a device. It analyzes competitive device offerings and tries to conceive of a better one. In many cases device plans work quite well. If a company is making just a simple addition to its product family, and the device is going to be sold only to existing customers, there is little need to do more.

At Intel we did lots of device planning, and usually we got away with it. That's because the devices were being developed to sell to the traditional customer base with the same sales force and distribution channels. Intel's corporate image was more than adequate to support those products.

If a product is going to be sold to the same market segment, a company can get away with merely training the sales force about the product's special characteristics and drafting a conceptually simple promotion plan. If, on the other hand, the product is going to a new market segment, at the very minimum the company must educate the sales force about the new customer base. The existing sales and distribution channels may also need reorganization. A new brand image may have to be established in the new market segment. Slight shifts in market segments require much more thorough plans: product plans. Device plans are inadequate. They will dramatically underestimate the levels of effort and the resources required to make the device successful in the new market.

In essence, a product plan consists of a device plan and a thorough marketing plan.

As the market segment gets farther and farther away from the ones the company traditionally serves, product plans become inadequate. *Business* plans are needed. Millions of dollars may be required to establish new sales and distribution channels, put in place the support infrastructure, and establish a brand image.

A lot of technology companies run into problems when they enter a new business without realizing it. A typical scenario develops as follows.

A great device is invented, which satisfies the needs of a totally new customer base. It requires new sales and distribution channels. But marketing doesn't budget to create them, so it falls back on the existing channels. The device then fails in the market, because the existing sales force does not have the time, skill, or motivation to call on the new customer base. The *device* never gets a chance to become a *product*.

Market segment changes are particularly insidious because of the unexpected stresses they can put on a company. When a firm develops a device to sell to an existing market segment, costs are frequently dominated by R&D expenditures. But when a company plans to enter a distant market segment, R&D costs are frequently dwarfed by market development costs.

Many technology companies either don't anticipate or ignore the costs of developing new market segments. They expect to spend $20 million to develop a new device, yet forget to budget $40 million for market development.

That is precisely what happened to Motorola during its initial efforts to enter the microprocessor business. The Model 6800, Motorola's first 8-bit microprocessor, was a fine device, but Intel beat it in the market place because Motorola had not made an adequate investment in training, in specialized salespeople, and in application support. By the time Motorola introduced the 68000, some of those problems had been corrected, but Crush never would have been as effective if the power of Motorola's distribution channels had matched the power of its devices.

Planning is hard work. As a matter of fact, planning can become an obsession, an avoidance mechanism. Some companies and individuals spend so much time planning, they never get on with the doing.

Other groups are guilty of underplanning. They plan devices when they should be planning products and plan products when they should be preparing business plans. Planning is worthless if directed at the wrong level.

THE BIGGER AND LONGER, THE GREATER THE RISK

Developing high-technology products takes longer and costs more than most companies anticipate. They are afflicted with "unkunks," the industry argot for unknown unknowns. An unkunk is a problem you are bound to have but can't anticipate. Unkunks are a primary cause of underestimated development schedules and costs.

The bigger a project, the bigger the errors, and the greater the number of unkunks. It isn't only defense contractors that make big mistakes, it is commercial companies as well.

Time is the deadly enemy of the technology business. Today's great idea is tomorrow's obsolete concept. The longer it takes a company to get its product to the market, the greater the likelihood a competitor will be there first.

Big plans with extended schedules are a risk in any business, but nowhere more so than in technology.

The riskiest plans are those with no interim product output. Developments that stretch over five years and promise a breakthrough at the end are very vulnerable. As the company withdraws into itself during the development, it can lose touch with the market. In the interim the market can even evaporate. That is happening to the many companies that developed "fail-safe" computers. Those programs took a lot longer than anticipated, and in the meantime the market changed to one in which the fail-safe feature is only one of many required. The companies did not realize that until it was too late.

PLAN FOR ACTION

A warning: In this increasingly sophisticated world of data bases and data analysis tools, it is a common failing for marketing people to confuse the plan with the result. They forget planning is a means to an end, not the end itself.

The purpose of planning is to make success more probable and to provide direction for the work that must be done. Plans seldom work unless the people involved in developing them are intimately involved in their execution.

A plan is a good one if it enables companies to focus their energies and achieve their goals. The only good plans are those that target commanding positions and then form the basis for achieving that result.

TEN

Great Products Need a Soul

GREAT MARKETING IS imaginative, analytical, and intellectual. But if that is all it is, it won't take a company far. Great marketing is also clever slogans, insightful product positioning, creative ads, and well-conceived devices. But if that too is all, a company will frequently be beaten.

The most important ingredients of great high-tech marketing aren't taught in business schools. Most marketing people don't even like to handle them. They require personal commitment to the product's success that is consistent with the company's philosophy, a dogged pursuit of customers, and an untiring commitment to service. Those are the soul of a product. With them a great product lives and grows, and even a weak product can endure against all odds.

When you think of it, the attitude required is not too different from that exhibited by great men and women who have overcome handicaps through a personal commitment and tedious pursuit of their goals. Commitment and perseverance enabled Teddy Roosevelt to overcome asthma, FDR his polio, and Kennedy chronic back pain.

What made Crush work, what is making Chrysler work, and what may enable Apple to battle IBM is more than just a superior product. It is belief in a cause. Without that belief most products will wither away—and the company is likely to follow.

Public relations won't work very well for soulless products. The press wants news, but it wants it from the people who make the news: the leaders, the men and women who inspire others to act. The press will listen intently, but unless the speaker comes across as confident, committed, and capable of not only convincing them but convincing the customer as well, even the best story will fall on deaf ears.

Ad agencies certainly won't tell you that in high technology, ads seldom sell products, people do. But it is true; no matter how effective the ad, the most it usually does is raise customer awareness and expectations. Salespeople and other employees must do the rest.

If you are going to win a marketing battle, if you are really going to overcome the odds, you need the support of everyone in the company. Only the inspiring commitment of a leader can deliver that. Obviously the sales force and distribution channels must be on the team. But so must the engineering group and the manufacturing organization. Once Crush was rolling at Intel, any employee we asked agreed to help. Engineers were willing to help sell to customers, even if they had other important projects. Manufacturing did the extra things to keep the customer happy. Even the personnel and finance departments got on board. It's true that those groups couldn't sell, but their interest and encouragement helped.

Every great marketing crusade has that kind of support. It is true at Chrysler. It was true at Avis. When it is time in your company to Crush the competition, every employee must want to play on the team.

Obviously, the most important group of all, the customers, must respond to a crusade as well. The same type of momentum that builds at football games when the underdog gains the upper hand takes place in the business world. Customers can begin to cheer for you as well. It happened in Crush: When customers saw the tide turning, they suddenly wanted to join the team, not leave it. Such outside enthusiasm is the best of all reinforcements. The press wanted to be the first to write about the victory, even before the battle was won. After all, who wants to be the second to report news?

Chrysler is enjoying this type of momentum today. For years the company was a joke. While reporters waited to write the Chrysler obituary, the press kept itself busy reporting on the progress of the disease.

No one today speaks of putting Chrysler out of its misery—just a few years ago a popular topic over business lunches. Now people want to emulate Chrysler. Customers are no longer "stupid" to buy

Chrysler cars, but "patriotic." The crusader who led it all is no longer the guy fired by Henry Ford; he is being discussed for the job of President of the United States.

Winning against the odds. Piling up the score so the competitor won't try again. Demoralizing competitors so they give up. Those are the jobs of marketing departments. It may not be pretty, but that is the sum and substance of marketing.

CRUSADERS NEEDED HERE

Some companies call them product managers. Business schools often have courses to train them. They are the people who run the PCs and prepare spreadsheet analyses of the various market strategies. They can tell you how much more product you will have to sell to make the same gross margin if you cut the price. They read market reports and analyze statistics. They are the people who segment the market and figure out what ads will appeal to which market segments.

The word "manager" implies someone who manages something. It means getting things done through people. Unfortunately, to many people wearing the title it connotes clean hands rather than working in the trenches.

It has been my experience that many individuals at technology companies flock to the product manager's job because it carries a lot of authority with very little responsibility. After all, when the success of a product is dependent on so many outside factors, who can blame the product manager for the failure?

In technology companies, product managers set prices, develop forecasts, and run promotion programs, but they don't control the sales force. They are frequently stuck with a product someone else defined long before they took their job. In truth, a product manager controls only a piece of his or her destiny. Because of that, many feel they do not own the success or failure of the product.

Some companies use the term "product champion." It is a term some clever marketing person must have come up with to appeal to the typical new college graduates fearful of the ethical implications of being in sales and marketing. "Champion" is a lovely word. It is clean-cut and healthy. It implies that if you train for the big event and work hard, you have a good chance of winning. It makes people think there is a set of rules all competitors will play by.

Unfortunately, the business world doesn't work that way.

Myself, I like the word *crusader* and all that word implies. The Crusaders were not nice people. They did some horrible things. They believed in their cause. They were willing to lay their lives on the line.

In business, when you run up against a crusader, you'd better be willing to fight just as hard as he or she does. Unfortunately for the product managers and the champions, there are lots of crusaders out there. I gave up a large portion of my life for Intel, and I am not unique in Silicon Valley. There are lots of people at Intel doing the same thing. And at AMD, Businessland, and Tandem.

There are rules in business, but they are few. I like to think of myself as a person of very high integrity. But I still did lots of tough things. Competitors never gave up as easily as they should. I would never have had to do what I did if they had simply accepted the inevitable.

The loss of any one of Intel's many battles with Motorola would have undermined the company's success and threatened my professional career. I put my corporate reputation on the line each time and Motorola did its best to ruin it. That is not the type of thing a clean-cut champion should do.

Actually, I have a great deal of respect for Motorola. It is a fine company and a good competitor. It plays by the rules. But competitors, even those that are reputable, do a lot of irritating and destructive things. Sure, competition makes for better business, but let's be truthful about it all: All business people would love to have the competition go away.

I once had lunch with K. K. Yawata, who was at the time the head of NEC's U.S. operations. Yawata is a fine man, but that did not change the way Intel felt about NEC. NEC is the largest semiconductor manufacturer in Japan. For years it had a very simple strategy for attacking Intel: Copy the Intel product line, give customers good service, and sell the copies at a very low price. In that way NEC could escape the costs of inventing products and developing markets. Instead, NEC could put all its efforts into manufacturing and service. At Intel we did not dislike NEC, we despised it.

Yawata told me a very interesting story that day over lunch. He explained that American companies didn't really compete like companies did in Japan.

"How is that?", I asked.

"To the death," he replied.

Now that was not a nice, friendly way to start a lunch—no matter who was paying.

I explained to K. K. that a number of companies in the United

States would love to compete in such a fashion, but the government took a very dim view of such practices. So, I continued, if a company drove every one of its competitors out of the business, it might end up the loser in court. I then gave Yawata a short history of American antitrust laws. Yawata seemed interested but definitely not impressed.

Anyone who competes with the Japanese should keep this story in mind. They play by their rules. When Japanese companies enter foreign markets, they conform to local rules and business practices. But if they can find a way to compete to the death, they will. That is precisely what our trade negotiators don't understand. The Japanese intend to drive their U.S. competitors out of business. They will play by their own rules as long as they can. Their rules are more favorable to them than our rules are to us. Needless to say, that does not concern the Japanese at all. They see it as merely a competitive advantage to be used in the war, a war that will go on until it is no longer to the advantage of the Japanese to fight it.

The Crush campaign was not nice, and that is one reason why it worked. The Intel salespeople were not nice, they were fierce competitors. They thrived on victory, on beating the other person. The peer pressure built up in the field over the Tahiti trip was not nice, but it made the less effective salespeople more aggressive. The Futures Catalog was accurate and fair, but it also was a strategic maneuver calculated to present an Intel strength while tricking the competitor into documenting its own weakness. When the competitor fell for the trick, we used its own catalog against it.

What we said and implied about our competitors during Crush wasn't always nice, but the facts were correct. It was important for customers to understand that Zilog did not have the resources to develop a complete product. We made sure customers were up to date on Motorola's problems and the difficulties its customers were having in using their devices. We tried not to "knock" our competitors—if only because that strategy can boomerang—but we most certainly found ways to let customers know the facts as we saw them.

From our point of view, our competitors were even more vicious, sometimes even unethical. Motorola ran its famous "benchmark" ads, which presented the 8086 in a very bad light. They were good ads, and if I could have run them I would have. Both Zilog and Motorola also spread rumors about Intel's plans to drop the 8086 in favor of a new super-microcomputer under development. The super-micro existed, but we had no plans to drop the 8086. Rumor mongering isn't against the law, but it isn't the sort of thing nice people do.

I wish I could look you in the eye and tell you how nice marketing is, but in all honesty I can't. If you have too many nice people in your marketing department and on your sales force, you are probably headed for trouble. If there are too many product managers and too many clean-cut product "champions" in your organization, chances are your balance sheet is going to suffer. If you plan to win, you should have a fair number of product crusaders on board. They are easy to spot. They're the ones with fire in their eyes and blood on their swords.

WHO SELLS PRODUCTS

Churchill "sold" Britain on its own ability to stand firm. Likewise, the foremost salesperson at Advanced Micro Devices is none other than Jerry Sanders, its president. At Intel, El Gelbach and I did a lot of high-level selling, but for the largest deals we always called on Andy Grove and Bob Noyce. The top salespeople are the top persons at many successful companies.

When it comes time to lead a really important product crusade, top management ought to be involved, especially when a business is young. Crush would not have been as effective without Noyce and Grove. A crusade requires the support of everyone in the company, but most of all the men and women at the top.

Crusades are extremely visible to the outside world. The press and the customers want to know if the company is really behind the effort. They may talk to the marketing people for a while, but they will remain unconvinced until they've checked out the story with the person "at the top." If he or she is unavailable (or worse, uninvolved), the story will never stick.

Of course, the president can't be the top salesperson for every project in the company. That's too bad. Fortunately for the president, a company can run only one big crusade at a time. He or she had better be involved it.

CRUSADES ARE ACTS OF LEADERSHIP

The original Crusaders made many of their conversions at swordpoint. That option is no longer open. It went out with the robber barons.

Nowadays, if a product is to succeed you must influence lots of people over whom you have no control. Customers seldom buy when they are ordered to. As a matter of fact, they become hostile when someone tries to tell them how to spend their money.

If customers are difficult, they are a cakewalk compared to the press. The press will listen attentively and even egg you on to make more and more extravagant claims about your crusade. Once you have really snowed them and dazzled them with blue smoke and mirrors, the press will have the nerve to hold you to your word.

The press is used to being lied to. Reporters are experienced in dealing with people trying to use them for their hidden ends. Once deceived, the press usually gets its revenge. Rightly so.

One reason why so many people get such bad press is that they immaturely try to get too much good press. They are constantly surprised the media didn't swallow their latest piece of hype. They forget that reporters who fall for too many phony stories lose their jobs. The gullible reporter is an extinct species at all great publications.

There are also numerous employees of the company who must dig in and support a crusade. Marketing can't order those people around either. Try it and you will find how busy they all become and just how protective their bosses can be. Yet all these groups are willing to be inspired and led. If the crusader believes, offers a rational hope, deals with them with conviction and honesty, and transmits his or her enthusiasm, then they will follow. They will become involved and will support the cause. All that is needed is leadership.

CRUSADES ARE FUN WHEN THE CONVERSIONS ARE EASY

Everyone likes to play on a winning team. Associating with a winner is fun. The momentum builds on itself. Recruiting members for a winning team is easy. People even fight to join.

Unfortunately, crusades are most needed not when things are going right but when everything is going wrong. If you want to find out who the real marketing people are in a company, gather your top employees in a room and ask who wants to volunteer to be the first over the hill in support of a losing cause. Only the very best will step forward.

Still, crusades will make good products more successful. When you have a real winner, a crusade can turn a victory into a rout. That is an opportunity that should not be missed. Whenever the rules let you annihilate a competitor, the laws of business survival dictate that you do so. After all, that competitor, if it can create its own crusade, will rise again.

Lots of people will crusade for a winning cause. Most people work best when surrounded by positive reinforcement. When they can feel the excitement in the market, and when the press flocks to them, the job is easy. When customers are praising the factory, when they are buying the product before it is even presented, and when distributors are racking up profits, crusading can be great fun. Every good marketing person should have a few of those. But you earn your spurs when the going is tough. Those are the times when great crusaders are needed most. These are the real corporate heroes: those who can lead in the tough times, who can fight the odds and win.

SELLING A DOG

A couple of years before the Crush campaign at Intel, I gave a management training course entitled "Selling a Dog." I did not realize it at the time, but I was describing a number of marketing crusades we had run at Intel. The process had always been the same.

The word "dog" is not a generally accepted marketing term. I define it this way: Dogs are products that are key to the company but are losing in the market place. Most companies have to deal with dogs at one time or another. The 8048 was a dog that went on to become the dominant product in its field. The 8080 was a dog too. With a lot of hard work, it won out as well. The Macintosh is Apple's dog. It is meeting only a few of the company's stated objectives and has not annihilated IBM.

Frequently great companies (and the not so great) have key products that are dogs. It does not matter whether the device is good or bad. What matters is that if the battle is lost in the market with those products, the company will lose its position in the market place.

At one time in my life, such a product would have demolished me. I would think: How could the company sell something that was not the very best? But that was before I understood what a "product" was. That was when I still believed that devices were products, before I understood that marketing was supposed to invent great products. And that was before I understood that no company can always have the best device.

The first dog I ever sold was the Hewlett-Packard 2116 minicomputer. If the product had failed, HP probably would not have become a force in the mini-computer business, and customers would have been deprived of a truly great supplier forever.

After I survived that crisis, I became more sanguine about the morality of the crusader style of marketing. Of course, you must be sure you want very badly to save a dog. Saving a dog product can be a very expensive effort. Not all dogs are worth it.

The crusade to save a dog product will not work unless it is of significantly greater magnitude than competitors' efforts to kill it. That means an intense focusing of considerable corporate resources on the program is required.

When you start digging into the problems associated with a dog product, the first thing you find is that the marketing department is whipped. The product managers have lost their killer instinct. The field sales force has often given up and is now selling other products. Why try to earn a living on commission by selling products the customer does not want? The salespeople and the product managers are commiserating about the horrible plight in which engineering and manufacturing have left them. Marketing has also carefully forgotten the key role it played in defining the product.

The first step in selling a dog is to find a crusader. The second is always to reexamine the market. Try to find the market segments where you can still win. Why do those segments like what you have? Why don't the others?

Resist the temptation to go after the whole market. Narrow your focus to the markets where you can win. Later you can expand your beachhead and take on the larger market.

Picking the easiest significant place to start is critical, because even winning there may be tough. Besides, you must gain momentum, and that takes victories. A few conquests, and morale will turn around. Only when your people know they can win should you consider waging a broader battle.

In essence, you must take an old device and create a new product for each market segment. In the case of the 8080, we tried to convince companies that the selection of the right microprocessor was the most important technical decision they would make in this decade. Intel's product then became not only the 8080 but Intel's entire product line. We could then sell our strengths: development support, application assistance, product reliability, the reduction in capital equipment required for the Intel product line, the size of our software group, our second sources, the twenty-seven other circuits in the product family, the training programs, and the credibility of Intel's management. The new product we invented had tremendous appeal.

The 8080 was a good device, but later ones developed by our competitors were better. But the 8080 remained the best product. When customers undestood that, they jumped on the Intel bandwagon. In the process of selling, we convinced ourselves as well that we had the better product, that the competitor was really offering the customer the weaker alternative. We rebuilt our own self-confidence, and we went on to win.

TOTAL MARKETING

Great marketing requires total commitment. You have to believe. You have to create. You have to sacrifice. You have to do battle. You have to win.

Great marketing—I call it *Total Marketing*—is a crusade. If you aren't strong enough to stay on the field, if you can't provide your product with a soul, you should find a nicer game to play.

ELEVEN

Do You Have Marketing?

A GREAT DEAL OF MONEY is wasted on marketing. Marketing budgets continue to grow. Yet seldom, if ever, do companies get what they are paying for. It is not that the money isn't needed—it usually is—but it's often spent unwisely.

Companies can finance a lot of marketing activity and still not have marketing programs. Ads can be run, press conferences held, sales calls made, data sheets and application notes published, competitive data collected, and the company still can be left with little to show for its efforts.

Why? Because the ads are carrying the wrong message, the press conferences are talking about the wrong subjects, and the application notes are describing irrelevant uses of the device.

Yet, to the untrained observer, each of those activities will appear to be competent, vigorous, and persuasive. The only contrary clue is that the programs are not achieving the desired results. There will always be a ready explanation, but the bottom line is that once a company commits to putting a device into the market place, marketing becomes responsible for turning that device into a product and making it a success. If it can't consistently do that, then you don't have marketing.

THERE ARE FEW REPEAT PERFORMANCES

Business schools have taught us how to collect data, and computers have made it possible to digest massive amounts of information. The world has become overwhelmed with statistical analyses, "what if" models, piles of computer printouts, and huge data bases.

Most businesses have become very skillful at gathering information about repetitive processes and then analyzing them to death. Data can now be captured on the factory floor and fed directly into a computer to analyze material flow, the quality of the various manufacturing processes, and the efficiency of execution at each production step. Other repetitive activities are subject to the same level of scrutiny.

Unfortunately, much of what is interesting in technology marketing is not repetitive, so a lot of the familiar tools won't help much. On top of this, a great many of the things marketing does are not subject to meaningful measurement. There are a lot of "one-shots" in marketing. You never have the chance to experiment as much as you would like.

For example, a product can occupy only one position in a market at any point in time. For many technology products, the life cycle is very short. If a product is positioned incorrectly, there may be no time to rectify the mistake before the product is obsolete.

The strategic side of marketing, which is a logical process, cannot be objectively measured. Statistics on the tactical portions of marketing may not be all that helpful either. The number of sales calls can be counted, but it is difficult to figure out from those data the effectiveness of the sales force. That's because some high-tech sales can take years. A salesperson may work for long periods to win a microprocessor design, and in the process may produce little computer-measurable output. The sale of a multimillion-dollar data processing system takes a very long time. During that period the salesperson has obviously made progress. But the evaluation of those efforts is purely subjective until the big order comes in.

There are, of course, a number of routine processes going on in any sales and marketing operation. These can be measured, and it is important to do so. The delivery to commitment, the order-processing throughput, the response time to service calls, and the mean time to repair are but a few examples. But, remember, all the measurable parameters can be going right and the marketing process can still be going wrong.

One of the best examples was the Great Semiconductor Boom of

1983–84. It was the shortest recovery and the quickest decline the industry ever experienced. In the winter of 1982–83 there were no orders to be had. Suddenly, the market turned on. The book-to-bill ratio (the ratio of orders received to product shipped) skyrocketed to more than two to one. Delivery times rapidly extended, and customers, concerned about product availability, placed orders covering periods extending beyond one year.

Now, no customer really knows how much it wants a year from now, but the semiconductor companies couldn't afford to turn down the orders, or they would be accepted by a competitor. Customers, in turn, couldn't afford not to get in line for products.

The boom of 1983–84 was caused by a jump in the PC business. The semiconductor manufacturers all knew that each of twenty PC companies was planning to capture an impossible 20 percent of the market. The problem was that we couldn't figure out which companies were going to win. It takes a great amount of arrogance to bet against the track records of companies like IBM, AT&T, HP, Olivetti, Wang, NCR, Univac, Compaq, ITT, Fujitsu, NEC, Convergent Technology, and Televideo.

We knew there was going to be a bust in the PC market. The real question was: When and how big?

Ultimately, the market turned down long before orders did. The hard data, the amount customers were ordering, did not reflect for months the serious problems those same customers were having with falling prices and wildly overstocked inventories.

Meanwhile it was almost impossible to get any valid information from the customers. Their purchasing agents still wanted as much of the product as they could get their hands on. The top managements all had reasonable justifications why they needed what they ordered and why they would be among the survivors. Our efforts to get them to cut back on orders were met with hostility. It was like asking a starving man to share his food.

The optimum strategy for the semiconductor companies at the time would have been to continue to take orders while cutting back on plant capacity. We all should have done that six months before the boom ended. But no one did. Morally and pragmatically, how could we? So instead, semiconductor manufacturers eventually were stuck with massive cancellations and a huge overcapacity.

Our hard data never showed what was really going on in the market. For that matter, our analysis of the hard data led to all sorts of erroneous conclusions. The gut feeling that Ed Gelbach, a senior vice-president of Intel, had about the situation was far more accurate than all the quantitative information the product managers generated. He called the market right, and the analysts called it wrong.

But people cling to hard data. The more of it there is around, the more they will believe it rather than their own feelings and impressions. It is tough to argue for instinct or intuition against numbers, even when you know much of the information is erroneous. And further, when you pay attention to data and they only pertain to the lesser factors, you frequently ignore the real problems.

Unfortunately, there is security in order and repetition. Human beings have powerful inclinations to reduce everything to numbers and multiple choice answers that can be fed into a computer.

I am convinced that surprisingly few important marketing insights are ever gained from these numbers. Many more come from keen observation—the human factor.

WHAT I LOOK FOR

Marketing is objective, intuitive, and subjective. Analysis is an important part of the creative process, but not the source of product invention, nor does it create marketing crusades.

I look for sixteen factors when evaluating a marketing program or a marketing department. I have found that if those factors are in place, most companies will be able to market successfully.

1. *Do programs comply with the "Strategic Principle"?*

Remember:

Marketing must invent complete products and drive them to commanding positions in defensible market segments.

Most companies fail because they never clearly identify the markets they are pursuing. Marketing departments can talk forever about the big market potential, but more often than not they are incapable of defining crisply the target market segment.

Only when a segment is identified can marketing departments talk specifics. They can then understand customer needs and develop programs to satisfy them. The marketing department will also know what has to be done to complete the product to beat the competition in that market. In short, they will be capable of planning and launching an assault that will capture a commanding market position and then of defending it.

Sometimes it takes years to get companies to define the markets they are really pursuing. I have continually watched marketing departments grapple with this problem in a number of technology companies.

The company that runs a good marketing program without good market segment definition and without a strategy to attain a commanding position is lucky, not skillful. A failure to define the target leads to very inefficient programs. Devices get enhanced and new features are added, but the device never becomes a complete product. Salespeople call on the wrong customers. Promotional programs are forever restarted and redirected. Turmoil reigns. In the end, someone else ends up with the commanding position.

2. Does marketing understand why customers will buy the product?

I recently talked with a marketing group that was demoralized and in complete disarray. The company had a fine product but had lost momentum in the market place. I asked a simple question of the marketing people in the room: "Why would a customer select your product over competitors'?" You could hear a pin drop.

No answer is the worst response of all. But it is surprising too how frequently the answers are naïve, illogical, and embarrassing. Ask that question. If you don't get good, simple, logical answers from all the individuals involved in promoting and selling the product, you have a problem.

Marketing people can't sell the customers on the product benefits if they don't know them. They can't communicate them if they are too complex.

3. Does a crusade mentality exist?

If a product is an important one, the company had better be on a crusade. If the product embodies new concepts for new markets, a

161

tremendous amount of work is needed to educate the customer base and develop the market. The individuals charged with that responsibility must create enthusiasm in the customer base, within the company, in the press, and in other influential publics. They can't do that unless they are committed and involved.

In an important market, the company is sure to face competition. The competitor, if it is competent, is going to attack the market with its own crusade.

Marketing is hard work. Enthusiasm, confidence, and commitment are infectious and are important ingredients in any product's success. If the crusade mentality is not there, the product will never reach its true potential.

4. Is customer satisfaction guaranteed?

A company's product is customer satisfaction. No company or product is going to succeed for long unless it delivers that satisfaction. In order to satisfy a customer, a product must be backed by the services a customer requires.

Many technology products are purchased by customers who have great expectations, only to have those expectations dashed. Sometimes the products fail to deliver their stated capabilities, and sometimes the products are too hard to use. The documentation may be poor, there may be insufficient applications support, or customer education programs may be inadequate. Frequently the quality of the new product is too low.

Unhappy customers are seldom repeat buyers. They also tell other people about their problems. It is very difficult to overcome bad word-of-mouth publicity.

Marketing departments should be able to explain why customers will get satisfactory utility from the product. They should understand the types of service customers require and be prepared to deliver them. If they can't do so, serious problems lie ahead.

5. Does the product match the sales and distribution channels?

It frequently does not. The product may be good in every respect, but there may be no good way to get it to the customer. The investment in building the necessary delivery system will often exceed the cost of developing the device. On top of that, it may take years to put in place an adequate sales and distribution network. One may not even be available to the company at any price.

That is precisely what the manufacturers of many of the IBM-compatible personal computers discovered when they went to sell their products. High-quality shelf space was simply not available.

Surprisingly enough, this problem tends to be ignored rather than confronted. By the time most companies come to grips with weak sales and distribution, it is too late. The time it takes to build the channels frequently exceeds the time to develop the device. That's why a well-prepared competitor who is late in the market can still wrest the market lead from the early participants.

Either the channels should already be there or the company should have realistic plans to build them. Without adequate distribution, no device can succeed.

6.   Will the promotion program work?

The first concern is whether the positioning for a product has ever been defined. Frequently the position is ill-defined or, worse, in conflict with the corporate goals. If the product has indeed been rationally positioned, the next question is whether or not that position is adequately reflected in the company's promotions.

A product's positioning should be the cornerstone of every piece of sales literature, advertising, and promotion. That is difficult to do if the position remains undefined until after the sales literature has been written, the advertisements produced, and the public relations tours run. Then it may be too late. The cost of starting over is too great.

Much of the effectiveness of any promotion depends on the creativity of the people involved. I know of no magic formula or advice that I can give on creativity other than to hire people who have it. When they are on board, and when the positioning framework is well thought out, the results are usually pretty good.

7.   Is the product different?

As stated before, I am always tempted to tell marketing people that "I would rather be different than better," knowing full well that if a product is truly different in some ways important to some customers, they will automatically perceive the product as better. Being different and offering customers features and services they cannot get anywhere else is one of the most important things a company can do.

Products succeed and become profitable when they are dramatically different in significant ways. Marketing departments should create differences and be capable of articulating their importance.

8. Does a marketing plan exist?

A marketing plan should exist. Sometimes it lives only in the head of a strong leader and is transmitted through his or her words and activities. But usually an unwritten plan is indicative of no plan at all. That's why I like to see plans written down.

Even then, it is not enough to have a written plan. It must be a living plan as well. The company must know it exists and must be following it. The plan should be continually reviewed. If the plan is written and never looked at again, it is not a plan at all.

9. Is pricing fair?

Admittedly this is a highly subjective question. No supplier–customer relationship lasts for long if the pricing is egregiously unfair. At the same time, no company can serve a customer well for long unless it earns a fair profit.

It is reasonably easy to determine if profit margins are adequate to sustain a company. This is an analytic job for the finance department. It is much more difficult to figure out whether the customer is being charged a fair price. So much of the customer's perception of fairness depends on the way the product is presented and the utility derived from it after purchase.

Marketing should be able to explain to management why the price is fair to both the customer and the company. If it can't do that, there is a good chance the company won't be able to explain it to the customer either.

10. Are the marketing programs integrated?

Dozens of activities take place in marketing. I am tempted to say hundreds. Companies have true marketing programs only when all pieces fit together. Too often the activities are disjointed. A promotion program exists but is not integrated with the selling process. A distribution program is in place but is in conflict with direct sales. Marketing departments must make the pieces fit together.

Managers should probe the most important programs and interfaces and assure themselves that they are compatible. The most significant disruptions occur between the marketing groups and the field organizations, between the promotions and other marketing groups, and between factory, engineering organizations, and marketing.

There are, of course, numerous other areas where programs and projects can get out of step. So many creative marketing people have so many good ideas that there is a tendency for individuals to do their own thing. In the end, the effectiveness suffers from incoherence in the market place. That can occur on items as simple as data sheets and press releases.

Unless all the ancillary activities are in step, the effectiveness of any product marketing program is bound to be impaired.

11. *Is marketing in touch with the customer base?*

Young marketing groups tend not to spend enough time talking with customers. The only way to find out what is going on out in the market place is to be there. That means making sales calls, visiting retail outlets, observing customer behavior, and listening to customers when they visit the factory.

There is a tendency to confuse the time spent presenting products to customers with the time spent gathering information from them. In order to be effective, marketing people must always be probing for information and building close relationships with customers.

The marketing groups that are really in touch with the customer not only can quote reams of data about the market but can also talk very specifically about the personality of the customer base. They will know customers by name and will be able to discuss their specific problems. They will be able to overwhelm you with examples. Important customers, key salespeople, and distributors will seek those marketing people out and will keep them informed about what is going on.

When such relationships exist, data take on meaning. Marketing departments then possess the specific information required to define complete products for market segments. They will know what the competition is doing and will understand the problems their own company is having servicing customer needs. Marketing departments are "in touch" when they know what their customers are thinking.

12. *Does marketing respect sales and vice versa?*

I have always been amazed by the number of marketing departments and sales organizations that don't get along. The complaints always seem to be the same: The sales organization isn't competent enough or sufficiently motivated to do the job, or the marketing department is out of touch with customers and wants to push the product into markets where it doesn't fit.

It really doesn't matter who is right. If that attitude exists, it is indicative of a severe management problem. It has to be fixed quickly. Either the product should be killed or the management problem solved.

I have seen good marketing departments take weak products and turn them into successes by owning up to the problem and working with the sales force to target the product on a niche where it can succeed. I have seen great devices starve because the field and the factory were at war.

Where there is real teamwork between sales and marketing, great products become more successful, and even the weaker ones can be made to succeed.

13. *Does marketing drive the organization?*

Marketing is a coupling of customer and company. It is the organization charged with understanding the market. It must drive the company to respond to the customer. Marketing is the organization that must make development groups aware of the customer's needs and the manufacturing organization knowledgeable about capacity and cost issues. Marketing must be active in planning the company's products.

Companies exist to satisfy the customer. It is a rare organization that will do so without a constant push from marketing. If the marketing group is not driving the organization to look after customer interests, who will?

14. *Are products managed throughout their life cycles?*

It is fun to deal with the hot new products. Usually great emotional and professional rewards are to be gained from establishing new markets and watching sales ramp up.

Less attention is paid to the more mature products. They need love too. When they don't get it, they die of marketing starvation or, worse, become problem children.

Good marketing departments are constantly aware of the status of the entire product line and manage both the new and old products throughout their life cycles.

15. *Is a forecasting system in place?*

No business stays the same for long. Unless there is a good forecasting system in place, problems are bound to be caused by changes in demand. If a business is underforecasted, significant opportunities may be lost. We are all familiar with the inventory problems caused by too much optimism.

It is extremely difficult to develop good forecasting systems. Customers never really know what they are going to buy, and salespeople are notoriously shortsighted in their outlook. Nevertheless, forecasts have to be made. A good forecasting process operates on a regular basis and makes use of the best specific customer intelligence available in both sales and marketing. With luck it will be right during periods of transition in the market.

16. *Does marketing have quality control?*

I have rarely seen quality control techniques extensively used in marketing organizations. It has become increasingly obvious to me, however, that marketing processes are amenable to the same quality control systems used elsewhere in a company.

In marketing departments, as in manufacturing organizations, there are really three types of functions. The first are repetitive functions that can be measured against absolute standards; second are regular functions whose evaluation is subjective; and third are those activities that occur at relatively random intervals.

If I had it to do all over again, I would have had a director of marketing quality control. I put one in place in our service organization at Intel, and he more than paid for himself. We also had a group devoted to measuring our delivery and administrative performance to customers. But, in retrospect, even that didn't go far enough.

There are numerous areas in marketing where it is easy to gather quantitative data. In product service you can easily measure the mean time to respond to a customer problem, the length of time it takes to fix that problem, and the number of repeat service calls that have to be made to fix the same problem. By the same token, in the marketing administration area one can compare performance to scheduled delivery, and paperwork accuracy.

Other areas of marketing should be perpetually audited. While it is nice to believe that management will make this part of its normal routine, in most cases pressure must be applied. At Intel, district service managers used to regularly visit accounts without the service engineer to determine customer satisfaction with the service support. Regular account reviews were held with our most important customers in order to determine their level of customer satisfaction.

But in spite of this, the process was hit or miss. We never achieved regular coverage of all important functions. Our process lacked the coherence that a well-run quality program should have.

I know this because we would constantly uncover field sales offices that could not handle their phone load. Andy Grove, the president of Intel, once became curious about our response time to literature requests and began auditing the process on his own. The response time improved dramatically. Happily, when Andy dropped his efforts, the literature group continued to audit its own performance.

I used to teach a marketing course in which I explained to new marketing people that marketing was a strategic and creative organization, but most important of all it was a service organization. Marketing was there to take care of customer needs and respond to customer requests. I would tell them that if they could not willingly and enthusiastically respond to their customers' requests, they were in the wrong profession.

Service to customers is measurable. It may not be as quantifiable as the "defects per million" in a manufacturing area, but is measurable enough. Lots of service organizations have found ways to monitor their quality. It is time marketing did the same thing.

MARKETING ACTIVITY IS NOT MARKETING

Most marketing people have very high energy levels. They are very good at explaining why anything they do is effective. When management looks at marketing, it is easy for it to come away dazzled by a slick presentation. After all, if marketing people can sell products, they ought to be able to sell their most important product, themselves.

If managers look behind the activity and ask just a few of the sixteen questions above, they will quickly determine whether they have marketing programs or marketing problems.

TWELVE

The Business of Business Is Total Satisfaction

IN 1960 THEODORE LEVITT argued that business makes a grave error when it perceives itself as producing products rather than satisfying customer needs. Here is one of his observations:

> Hollywood barely escaped being totally ravished by television. Actually, all the established film companies went through drastic reorganizations. Some simply disappeared. All of them got into trouble not because of TV's inroads, but because of their own myopia. As with the railroads, Hollywood defined its business incorrectly. It thought it was in the movie business. "Movies" implied a specific, limited product. This produced fatuous contentment which from the beginning led producers to view TV as a threat. Hollywood scorned and rejected TV when it should have welcomed it as an opportunity to expand the entertainment business.*

The TV industry had a need, and the motion picture companies had the product. They missed the opportunity.

There are countless examples of myopic, and ultimately suicidal, corporate behavior. The transistor did in the vacuum tube business; the inexpensive calculator put an end to slide rules; semiconductor memory toppled the magnetic core manufacturers, and on and on.

*Theodore Levitt, "Marketing Myopia," *Harvard Business Review,* July-August 1960; also in *The Marketing Imagination* (New York: Free Press, 1986), pp. 141–172.

Customer needs did not go away, but the optimal way of satisfying those needs changed.

The static and dying industries of America are not the only ones suffering from marketing myopia. Many dynamic high-tech companies are afflicted with the same disease. Most of the mainframe computer companies never successfully made the transition to mini-computers, and most mini-computer companies missed out on PCs. In the semiconductor industry, a rash of new companies popped up to exploit exciting new market niches in semicustom and custom circuits just at the time when everyone thought the semiconductor business was too expensive to enter. Those niches turned out to be very important, and the little guys have captured the lead from the giants.

Marketing myopia is a dangerous disease. It attacks those who are not constantly searching for better ways to serve their customers' needs. And it is easily contracted in rapidly changing environments.

Twenty-three years later, Levitt proposed a definition for *corporate purpose:*

1. The purpose of a business is to create and keep a customer.
2. To do that you have to produce and deliver goods and services that people want and value at prices and under conditions that are reasonably attractive relative to those offered by others to a proportion of customers large enough to make those prices and conditions possible.
3. To continue to do that, the enterprise must produce revenue in excess of costs in sufficient quantity and with sufficient regularity to attract and hold investors in the enterprise, and must keep at least abreast and sometimes ahead of competitive offerings.
4. No enterprise, no matter how small, can do any of this by mere instinct or accident. It has to clarify its purpose, strategies, and plans, and the larger the enterprise the greater the necessity that these be clearly written down, clearly communicated, and frequently reviewed by the senior members of the enterprise.
5. In all cases, there must be an appropriate system of rewards, audits, and controls to assure that what's intended gets properly done and, when not, that it gets quickly rectified.*

Levitt's words are an eloquent and profound statement about the purpose of an enterprise. They go far beyond the trite notion that businesses exist only to make money.

*Theodore Levitt, *The Marketing Imagination* (New York: Free Press, 1986), pp. 5–6.

171

WHAT IS THE PRODUCT OF BUSINESS?

We are surrounded by the skeletons of dead businesses. Some have been killed by competitors. But most simply lost their way and starved for lack of orders or because the price of their services and products had sunk below a level at which they could earn a fair return.

Many of the industries in America's rust bowl are in trouble. Semiconductor companies have lost dynamic RAM market share to the Japanese. The electronic game business is winding down. Large numbers of minicomputer and PC companies have vanished.

The problem is not unique to the United States. Companies in Europe, Japan, and other Far East countries are all feeling the crush of increased competition. The steel and shipbuilding industries are on the ropes in Japan. Many of Europe's great companies are now mere shells protected by governments rather than by their own viable products.

There are always lots of reasons why companies and industries die. It is always easy to blame someone else for your problem. The labor unions got too much money, or the work force wasn't reliable enough, or the competition was unfair, or the management was bad. But from the customer's point of view, the reason is always the same: *Companies fail because they are incapable of delivering total customer satisfaction.*

The way the customer sees it, someone else's price or quality is better. Perhaps it got better service from a competitor, or the supplier did not keep up with the new technology. Or maybe tastes changed, or the customer just wanted something different. For whatever reason, the customer went away.

It has always been incredible to me how insensitive companies can be to their customers. Most of them don't seem to understand that their future business depends on having the same customer come back again and again.

Every business should regularly ask itself the question "Will my customer come back?" Apparently, many never do. If they did, grouchy supermarket checkout clerks, dirty service station rest rooms, discourteous salespeople, shoddy products, poor documentation, and exploitive pricing would not exist. But they do. They can be found even in potentially fine institutions that do not fully understand the real product of their business.

Every business I can think of depends on repeat customers. People, of course, can be in a hula hoop kind of business and make money. But after a while there are no repeat customers. If hula hoops are all those people make, then they are not in business any longer. There will always be one-shot opportunities where someone can open a storefront and vanish the next day. I don't call that a business. Real businesses depend on customers coming back.

I am not a K-mart customer. I shop there approximately once a year. If K-mart depended on me and others like me they would be out of business. But K-mart does have millions of regular customers, and it had better keep those customers happy with the products they purchase. Intel had thousands of customers, but two hundred of them and about ten distributors constituted more than 90 percent of the sales volume. So it was very easy to figure out whom Intel had to keep happy. The health of Intel's business was extremely dependent on the satisfaction and vitality of a very few customers. If you analyze your business, you may be surprised as well at how few customers make up 90 percent of your sales.

Most of us are regular customers—somewhere. We continue to return to the same stores. We go time and time again to the same restaurants. Ask McDonald's. We find brands we like and continue to purchase them. Companies are no different. They have certain vendors they prefer to do business with. They become dependent upon those vendors.

When a customer comes to trust a supplier, it is extremely difficult for a competitor to steal that customer away. Customers don't want to leave IBM. Often they can't afford to. In the semiconductor industry, a big customer that can depend on a supplier's performance and quality can save millions of dollars in inventory, manufacturing costs, and capital. Thus a switch to another vendor entails a big risk and is very expensive. A satisfied customer will think twice before he makes a move.

At Intel, we knew who the good vendors were and whom we couldn't count on. We were prepared to devote our energies to doing business with a few very good suppliers we could trust. Why not? It saved a lot of money and led to even better service. After all, we reasoned, when you depend on someone, they become dependent on you as well, and things are bound to get better and better.

Most businesses depend on a relatively few happy customers for their livelihood. Even those that apparently have a very large customer base are usually highly dependent on a small percentage of that population. If those customers are happy and successful, their key vendors are likely to prosper as well.

Customers are a very scarce commodity, especially good ones. Any technology salesperson or marketing manager worth his or her salt can rattle off a list of good customers from memory. Good customers are hard to create. It often takes years to make a customer really dependent on you. Once the relationship has been created, it is easier to maintain. But it still takes a lot of work.

Your competitors know who the good customers are, too. Any competent competitor makes its living building its own customer base and "stealing" from yours. That's what helps keep both of you honest.

If the purpose of business is to create and hold customers, then the product of business must be *total customer satisfaction*. Satisfied customers have had their needs met time and time again. Unfortunately, there are not many businesses in this world capable of delivering total customer satisfaction. How many of your suppliers are you really happy with?

Suppliers need not suppress their own needs to satisfy a customer. A supplier has to earn a fair profit. A good customer understands its vendor's needs and has that firm's interests at heart. Good customers don't make unreasonable requests. After all, they want to create and hold good suppliers as well.

WHAT FITNESS REQUIRES

Yankee ingenuity has been the cornerstone of U.S. industry. Thomas Edison told the employees of General Electric to find a need and fill it. Everywhere one looks, one sees great American inventions and the industries they created. The transistor, the integrated circuit, the electronic computer, the supermarket, the Big Mac, and thousands more are all the creations of great minds searching for new ways to "fill needs."

America is also a country obsessed with the next great invention. The large number of cases of marketing myopia afflicting the industrial structure of the country is the result of that obsession. The new keeps displacing the old.

Companies supplying products satisfying customer needs do not suffer from marketing myopia. They are constantly searching for better ways to solve customers' problems, even it if means parting with the tried and true. They move with the ebb and flow of tastes. They are constantly searching for new products and services while continuously modifying old ones. They are striving to invent complete products meeting the criteria for "fitness for needs."

Technology companies, in their haste to be "state-of-the-art," rarely pay enough attention to "fitness for customer needs." Unless they do, they will never deliver total customer satisfaction. Most business strategy sessions I have attended in technology companies talk about devices and deal with micro issues. I have seldom seen a session start with a discussion of the customers a company wants to create and hold—even though that issue is the key to a company's future. I have seldom heard these questions asked: "What customers are most critical to the company?" "What must we do to hold them?"

In a multidivisional company such questions are almost never raised. After all, it is reasoned, the customers belong to the company and not to the division. Besides, few division product managers understand their company's overall business strategy. If it exists, often no one has told them. Instead they see their job as optimizing the sales and profits of their division. It would be rare indeed to hear a division manager make a presentation espousing the milking of his product line so that the company could get into a new business to satisfy a customer need. Sometimes, in fact, division profit centers can act as marketing inertia centers.

That is why top management should be involved with the company's most important customers and involved in strategic planning. Only then will it appreciate what must be done to retain and expand the customer base and gain a competitive advantage. Top management should be among the foremost authorities on the market segments the company is serving. It should be able to convey that knowledge to the product managers, not vice versa. After all, top executives are the people who can ask the big questions and make the big decisions. Only the man at the top can decide to take profits from one business to build another or even to sell a business to acquire the resources to build a new one. Product managers haven't that power or perspective.

A company dedicated to "fitness for customer needs" must commit itself to new product invention, modification, and a willingness constantly to refocus its business resources to satisfy those needs. Companies that do all of that will not suffer from marketing myopia. They will have the resources to stay in their markets. If the resources are there and are coupled with the proper level of intellectual curiosity and inventiveness, the company's success should be assured. Right?

Well, no. Too many companies have relied on the new to assure their success in business. The conventional wisdom in many technology fields is that companies should invent so fast that competitors can never catch up. It was believed that the way to deal with the Japanese, Koreans, Taiwanese, and big domestic competitors was to put them on a technology treadmill so they could never catch up. So technology companies watched those "ogres" copy their older products and relinquished the markets to them while they went on to invent the new. That happened in office copiers, typewriters, floppy disc drives, and semiconductors, to name but a few.

But the small high-tech firms didn't count on one thing: The big domestic competitors and the Japanese kept getting smarter. So did the Koreans, the Taiwanese, and the Brazilians. The time needed to copy kept growing shorter and shorter, and the copies got better and better. Pretty soon a number of the laggards had caught up. Then they started to invent. The profits earned from the good copies were used to finance the next round of invention. All of a sudden, the strategy of just running faster did not work so well and was not nearly as attractive.

Companies have come to realize that keeping customers involves more than endless invention. The new is not enough. You also need execution. In industry after industry, the Japanese and others have stolen secure leads by focusing on excellence in execution.

That of course has not always been the case. Postwar Japan sold cheap goods, and the words "Made in Japan" stamped on a product in the 1950s were synonymous with low quality. Anyone who played with the Japanese toys knew they always broke. Fortunately, a good many of the Japanese products were targeted at kids with attention spans shorter than the mean time to product failure, a perfect match of product to market segment.

The Japanese coupled quality of execution with one other very important ingredient: low price. Cutthroat pricing is always a terrific way to steal mature customers. The best-for-less sales pitch has always worked, especially when you can deliver on the promise.

Never mind that the Japanese were "unfair" and used cheaper labor and lower-cost capital. We are now talking about keeping customers. Firms will always be won over by the best-for-less argument, even when they don't want to (like American and European firms buying from the Japanese), because if they don't, a competitor will gain an important advantage.

Quality programs at first focused on the existing product and improved what was already there. Initially that orientation was internal and concerned itself with building better and better devices. With the advent of total quality control, defined as "fitness for use," it has spread to the customer interface as well. It now concerns itself with the quality of all the products, interfaces, and services being offered.

But there is another side to all this. Perhaps the Japanese emphasis on improving and refining existing products and processes in part explains the problems they have had in inventing new products and services. After all, always asking how to improve the quality of a semiconductor ROM will not lead to the invention of the EPROM. Nor will trying to improve the quality of an integrated circuit inspire a company to invent the microprocessor.

The weakness in trying to satisfy customers' needs through quality of execution alone is the same one Levitt identified in "Marketing Myopia." While the need endures, the product used to satisfy the need changes. For example, when customers' tastes change and they want to pay more to buy their clothes in a boutique, the very basis of a department store's merchandising concept is threatened. Those stores choosing to retain this segment of their customer base have had to redesign their retail product. They put boutiques in their department stores.

So the weakness with using total quality control to drive a business is that it doesn't force one to invent new products and services. And you can't forever satisfy the needs of technology customers without invention.

American technology companies have always led in innovation. The genius of American business lies in risk-taking, creativity, invention, and ambition. But those qualities alone are not enough. The future of technology requires a rekindling of the traditional American values as well: the work ethic, attention to detail, and the commitment to excellence.

Fortunately, when one looks in American industry these days, one sees a commitment to "fitness for use" growing. A wave of enthusiasm is sweeping this country, from workers to managers, to do a job right the first time. Most important, the customers themselves are demanding quality of execution. They see it as a vital part of the products they buy. And when the customers demand it of their suppliers, those vendors will deliver it.

We are in a race for high-tech survival, a race between nations using cheaper labor, operating under "unfair rules," and struggling to instill inventiveness in their industries; and the United States, where high-tech companies, forged in the crucible of invention, must now recommit themselves to the American heritage of high quality and pragmatism.

In this increasingly competitive environment, companies must struggle against greater and greater odds to create and keep customers. To accomplish that, they have no choice but to commit themselves to delivering total customer satisfaction, products that meet the criteria of "fitness for needs."

The great high-tech companies will continue to invent and innovate at an ever-increasing rate. The ongoing explosion of technical knowledge, spurred on by the desire to taste victory, to rise above their neighbors, and to avoid the pain and anguish of defeat, will continue to drive these companies. When this inventive genius is then supported by a corporate superstructure committed to total quality control, the ultimate "complete products" that emerge will be invincible in the market place. The institutions building those products will prosper and grow.

When you survey the diversity of new products on the market, you cannot help but be overwhelmed by their variety. But in truth though, their variety obscures the fact that the great companies spewing forth this bewildering array of choices are delivering only one thing: total customer satisfaction. If you aspire to be great, let that be your goal.

APPENDIX A

The Cost of Attacking
a Competitor

GREAT MANY THINGS create barriers to market entry. One could spend many years figuring out what all of them are for any business. However, much of what a company needs to know can be arrived at quickly by making a few rough estimates.

What I would like to do here is to show you how I arrived at my estimate that the barriers to market entry were equal to about 70 percent of the forecast sales of the leader. This will have to be done by example, as there is no way to derive the number from theory. I suspect that a similar analysis of most industries would come up with numbers that are very close. For purposes of this discussion, I am going to use a computer type of business, with which I am intimately familiar.

The way I developed the rule of thumb was to estimate the investment required to establish a market presence and distribution channels, develop a product line, and provide the necessary capital for plants, equipment, inventory, and working capital. The estimate of investment in the sales and marketing area was derived by looking at the costs of establishing a sales force and equipping the field with spares and demonstration units, and making an educated guess of the costs associated with building a brand image, developing customer support functions, and providing documentation. The development costs for the product line have been estimated by doing a simple analysis of cumulative development costs as a percentage of sales.

A successful computer company in the end-user computer business sells about $1 million per salesperson per year. If it achieves $500 million in sales, it must have about five hundred salespeople on board. Each salesperson costs about $100,000 a year to support. As a rule of thumb in the industry, a salesperson is about 50 percent productive in his or her first year. The training costs for this type of professional are therefore $50,000. That means the company would have spent about $25 million training the sales force if there was no turnover in the organization. If the turnover in the group over the years was in the range of 20 to 40 percent, the training investment would increase to between $30 million and $35 million, or about 6 to 7 percent of the $500 million in sales. That is only the cost of building the sales force.

Every company uses capital for financing inventory, plant, and equipment. A large percentage of the assets employed are unique to the business in which the company participates. A portion of the remainder is committed to inventories and equipment that may be dedicated to a product line.

If a company earns a profit after tax (PAT) of 10 percent and a return on assets (ROA) of 15 percent, then:

$$PAT = \frac{Profit}{Sales} \times 100\% = 10\%$$

$$ROA = \frac{Profit}{Assets} \times 100\% = 15\%$$

And therefore:

$$\frac{Assets}{Sales} = \frac{PAT}{ROA} = \frac{10\%}{15\%} = .67 = 67\%$$

The portion of assets committed to spares inventory to service complex equipment may be on the order of 2 to 5 percent of a company's sales. Frequently a company will have one demo unit for every twenty to fifty units sold in a year, making the investment in demo equipment fall in the range of 1 to 3 percent of sales, depending on the gross margin of the product line. Therefore, assets equaling between 3 and 8 percent of sales are committed to the marketing area.

Miscellaneous costs of developing a market presence, documentation, and customer training are cumulative, and the start-up costs and losses associated with introducing a new product requiring extensive postsale support in the field probably amount to a few percentage points. A reasonable guess for those miscellaneous expenses in a computer-like business is that they will run 5 to 10 percent of the final year's sales.

If a company is growing at a rate of 30 percent a year and spends 10 percent on R&D, then it will have spent, over a four-year period, an amount equal to about 30 percent of the fourth year's sales in developing and enhancing the product line.

On top of this, complementary businesses often develop around the leading competitors. These businesses supply services the customer base needs. They are unavailable to the new market entrant. It must frequently invest itself to develop products its competitor got free. Independent software vendors (ISVs) supplied much to the software to make the IBM PC a success. Intel, by encouraging the growth of niche market multibus suppliers, was able to offer its customers a much more complete product line. Leading semiconductor suppliers can frequently charge large royalties for licensing their parts, while incremental suppliers are forced to give away their technology to gain support in the market.

The investment the leader has in establishing his position in the market as a per cent of his fourth years sales is very roughly:

Assets	(%)
Spares inventory	2–5
Demonstration equipment	1–3
Other assets	61
Total	*64–69*
Product development	30
Developing channels of distribution	6–7
Miscellaneous marketing	5–10
Total investment	*105–116*

Even though the above calculation is extremely rough, it does point out a number of things. The first is that the leader has invested on the order of a dollar for every dollar of sales. That is consistent with rules of thumb used in many businesses. For capital-intensive businesses, it is low. In the semiconductor field, companies like Intel are making capital investments on the order of one dollar for every dollar increase in sales. Working capital is required in addition to that number. Forgetting about the "other assets" in the table, i.e., the money required for plants, inventories, accounts receivable, and so forth, the investment the leader has in other things unique to his business is probably on the order of 43 to 55 percent of his sales.

It is extremely uncomfortable to be competing directly with a competitor who is twice your size. He always seems to have the products there first and to have more of them. No wonder—he is probably spending twice as much on developing his product line. He seems always to get to the customer first. That follows as well, since he will probably have twice as many salesmen or stronger distributors. Therefore, any plan based on a head-on attack should strive to get to at least 70 percent of the leader's size. That means a company should plan on investing an amount equal to about 70 percent of the leader's investment.

The market share a company must have to be effective in a market is to a great degree determined by the market share of the leader. If a follower is going to equal 70 percent of the leader's market share, and if a leader has 50 percent market share, the follower should plan on having 35 percent. If the leader has only 20 percent, the follower can live with about 15 percent.

Admittedly no two companies are the same. In all likelihood they have products that are somewhat different, so they are probably serving market segments that are in some way different. In some cases you may therefore see a leader with a large market share and successful competitors with substantially less. When that is the case, it is probably because of the immaturity of the market or because the smaller competitors have found niches to serve.

If the cost of entering the market against an entrenched competitor is 70 percent of its projected sales at some point in the future, it follows that the cost of crossing the barriers to enter a market is probably in the range of

$$\text{cost of market entry} = (.7) \times (\text{leader's market share}) \times (\text{size of market})$$

On close examination, this formula explains why it is possible for small companies to enter new markets that will become large when there are no major entrenched competitors. However, once a market has grown to a good size, even though it is still immature, and has a leader with even a 20 percent market share, entering the market becomes an investment as well as an invention game.

All companies must make large investments to establish themselves in the market place. The capital must be raised in equity markets, earned on sales, or borrowed. For late entrants, the opportunity to earn profits when they have a small percentage of a large market is seriously limited. Therefore, companies should plan on large capital infusions from the other sources.

If you don't have deep pockets, don't try. Be different, pursue market segments, but don't attempt a head-on assault.

APPENDIX B

How Costs and Margin Goals Affect Price

SURPRISINGLY, SMALL DIFFERENCES in costs and margin objectives have dramatic effects on the price a company must command in the market place.

The reader can derive the formula for the price differentials. But for two manufacturers making the same product where CH is the cost and COGH is the percentage cost of goods sold for the high-cost manufacturer and CL and COGL are the same variables for the lower-cost supplier, the percent of price differential is:

$$\text{percent price differential} = \left(\frac{CH}{CL} \times \frac{COGL}{COGH} - 1 \right) \times 100\%$$

For example, in a typical quasi-commodity business such as printers, disc drives, or electric components, a Japanese supplier may operate at 35 percent gross margins or 65 percent cost of goods. Because it may use a follower strategy, it will operate with lower R&D and marketing costs. The lower salary structure for professionals in Japan has a further positive effect on those costs. Also, because of the lower cost of capital, a Japanese company may be able to get by with 5 percent pretax profits. All of those factors make gross margins that are unacceptably low by American standards reasonable in Japan.

Index

Advanced Micro Devices (AMD), 17, 45, 152

Advertising, 33, 34, 50–51, 99; *see also* Copy; Promotions

Airline industry, 114

Apple, 2, 24, 31, 51, 140, 147, 154
Lisa, 75
Macintosh, 43–44, 154

Arrow Electronics, 60–61

Automotive market, 14–15, 120

Avis Rent-a-Car, 2, 90, 96, 148

Bader, Rich, 4

Barrett, Craig, 54

"Beltway Bandits," 107

Bipolar microprocessor, 25, 26

Borovoy, Roger, 5

Boston Consulting Group, 13–14

Brand image, 38

Brazil, 132

Buckout, Don, 4

Busicom, 25

Business plans, 143, 144

Businessland, 97–98

Caterpillar Tractor, 42

Chrysler Corporation, 2, 32, 50, 90, 94, 147, 148

Co-destiny, 65, 109–110

Compaq, 47

Complete products, 139, 165

Complexity of high-tech products, 27–28

Computer-aided engineering (CAE) equipment, 114–115, 122, 139

Computer industry, 28, 31, 37–38, 62, 71–74, 83, 92, 93, 159–160, 171

Computerland, 98

Control Data Corporation (CDC), 21

Copy (advertising), 89–90

Corning, 128

Corporate culture, 49–50

Corporate purpose, 171

Cosby, Bill, 25

Cost–price relationship, 104–106, 184–185

Costs of products, 34–35

Crusader style of marketing, 147–156, 161–162

Crush campaign (Intel), 5–11, 91, 145, 147, 148, 151, 152

Currency fluctuations, 129

Customer base, evolving, 30–32

Customer satisfaction, 162, 168, 170–178

Daisy (engineering company), 62–63

Dataquest, 138

Davis, Bob, 104

Death spiral pricing, 38

Decisive competitive advantage, 35–36

Delegation of responsibility, 4

Deliveries, accurate, 58–59

Device emulation, 26

Device plans, 143–144

Diamond, Jerry, 130, 131

Differentiation
advertising and promotion, 50–51
corporate culture and, 49–50
distribution channels and, 45–47
intangibles and, 47–48
product, 37–44, 163–164
salespeople and, 44–45
service and, 48–49

Digital Equipment Corporation (DEC), 16–17, 21, 62, 67, 72

Digital telephone networks, 121

Direct mail, 99

Discounts, 73

Distribution, 45–47, 74, 75, 162–163
  hidden cost of, 85–88
  knowledge and functions of, 75–78
  specialized, 21, 78–81, 88
  supporting, 81–85
Distributor margins, 85–87, 112
"Dog" products, 154–156
Drug industry, 78
Durango Systems, 88

Early adaptors, 30
Edison, Thomas, 174
80/20 rule, 64
Electronic distribution, 60–61, 86–87
EPROM (erasable programmable read only memory) chip, 2, 136–137
Experience curves, 13, 14

Fail-safe computer industry, 138–139, 146
Failure analysis, 124–125
Fairchild 3870 microcomputer, 43, 135, 136
Fanuc, 124–125
Follower strategy, 22, 23
Ford Motor Company, 48
Ford Mustang, 18, 32
Forecasting, 167
France, 118
Fujitsu, 2
Future Shock (Toffler), 93

Garrow, Bob, 16
Gelbach, Ed, 152, 159–160
General Electric Company, 14, 22, 28, 62, 71, 137, 174

General Motors Corporation, 18
Giroud, Bernard, 130
Gray market, 107–108
Great Semiconductor Boom of 1983–84, 158–160
Grenier, Jim, 56
Grove, Andrew, 2, 4, 7, 11, 55, 152, 168

Hamilton-Avnet, 60–61
Hewlett-Packard Company, 38, 39, 42, 50, 71, 111, 112, 123, 128, 140
  2116 computer, 71–74, 154–155
High-technology products
  definition of, 28–30
  distribution channels, 46–47
  marketing differences, 32–34
Hitachi, 2
Hoff, Ted, 25, 26, 137
House, David, 4, 9

Iacocca, Lee, 2, 4, 32, 48, 50, 90, 94, 149
IBM Corporation, 9, 10, 42, 45, 49–50, 62, 71, 100, 115, 122, 147, 173
IBM PC, 31, 38, 39, 96
ICE module, 54
In Search of Excellence (Peters and Waterman), 53
Innovators, 30
Intangibles, 42, 47–48, 93
Integrated marketing programs, 164–165
Intel Corporation, 2–11, 15–17, 21, 23, 25–26, 38–40, 43, 48, 54–56, 62, 64–65, 67, 77–79, 86, 87, 91, 100, 106, 111, 123, 124, 127, 130–131, 134–138,

Intel Corporation (*continued*)
  140, 143–145, 150–152, 168,
    173
  8008, 102
  8031, 107–108
  8048, 43, 135, 136, 154
  8080, 9, 26, 102–103, 115,
    154–156
  8086, 3, 4, 6, 8, 94, 124, 151
  8088, 3
  80186, 96, 103–105, 114
International markets, 118–132
  corporate controversy and,
    124–126
  currency fluctuations and market
    share, 129
  management problems of,
    130–132
  nationalism, cost of in, 128–129
  reasons for presence in, 119–123

"Japan Inc.," 96
Japanese industry, 13, 19, 22, 23,
    49–51, 59–60, 63, 96, 105,
    118, 120–129, 132, 150–151,
    176–177
Jobs, Steve, 51
Joint ventures, 128

Katz, Jeff, 4
Kay, David, 112
Kaypro, 112
K-mart, 173
Kodak, 67
Korea, 118, 122, 128
Kroc, Ray, 32

Lally, Jim, 4, 5, 9, 11, 16
Lamb, Frank, 41
Late adaptors, 30–31

Leadership, 22
  promotions and, 100–101
  service and, 66–67
Levitt, Theodore, 170, 171, 177
Life cycles, product, 167
Local manufacture, 125
Logistical systems, 60–61

Maintenance, 58
Manufacturing flexibility, 59–60
Market basket approach, 84
Market entry barriers, 17, 19–22,
    51, 141, 179–183
Market positions, price and,
    111–112
Market segmentation, 14–25, 29,
    35–36, 160–161, 165
  creation of, 18–19
  defined, 17–18
  entry barriers, 17, 19–22, 51,
    141, 179–183
  planning and, 138–140
  service and, 63–64
Market share, 13–15, 28; *see also*
    Market segmentation
Marketing department, support of
    sales and distribution
    channels, 81–82
Marketing Imagination, The
    (Levitt), 171*n*
Marketing invention, 32
Marketing myopia, 170–171, 174,
    175
"Marketing Myopia" (Levitt),
    170*n*, 177
Marketing plans, 164
  defined, 142–143
  types of, 143–144
Marketing program, factors in
    evaluation of, 160–169
McDonald's, 32, 173
McKenna, Regis, 4, 9, 10, 11, 92

Microcomputer, invention of, 25–26

Miller Lite Beer, 18, 91

Moore, Gordon, 2, 55

Mostek, 135

Motorola, 2–6, 8–11, 91, 122, 135, 145, 150, 151
  6800, 26, 145
  68000, 145

Multibus, 16–17

National Semiconductor, 2, 3, 16, 46–47

Neiman-Marcus, 49–50

Niches, 28

Nippon Electric Corporation (NEC), 2, 16, 150

Noyce, Robert, 2, 7, 25, 26, 48, 130, 152

Olivetti, 28

Overdistribution, 76, 112

Pacific Basin market, 122, 126, 128

Packard, Dave, 7

Pan Am, 63

Partial products, 27, 28

Patents, 141

PC market, 31, 37–39, 96, 159–160

Perspectives on Experience (Boston Consulting Group), 13

Peters, Tom, 53, 70

Philips Company, 2

Pioneer, 112–113

Planning, 133–146
  for commanding positions, 140–141

market segments, identification of, 138–140

marketing plan, defined, 142–143

marketing plans, types of, 143–144

Polaroid, 67

Positioning of products, 91–95, 97, 100, 101, 163

Powell, Casey, 4, 11

Press, the, 153

Pricing, 102–117, 164
  co-destiny relationship and, 109–110
  device versus product, 106–107
  distribution and, 112–113
  market positions and, 111–112
  price–cost relationship, 104–106, 184–185
  subjectivity of, 113–117
  "what the market will bear" concept, 107–108

Product, defined, 27

Product costs, 34–35

Product differentiation: *see* Differentiation

Product life cycles, 167

Product managers, 149

Product plans, 143, 144

Product positioning, 91–95, 97, 100, 101, 163

Product specifications, 124

Promotions, 50–51, 89–101, 163
  international, 127
  leadership and, 100–101
  as part of process, 99–100
  product positioning, 91–95, 97, 100, 101
  simplicity and, 96–98

Quality control, 55–57, 167–168, 177

RCA Corporation, 28
Repetition in promotions, 97, 98
Rockwell, 122, 137
   PPS-8, 26
Rosen, Ben, 2

Sales calls, 99
Sales channels
   knowledge and functions of,
      77–78
   specialized, 78–81, 88
   supporting, 81–84
Salespeople, 44–45, 71–75; *see also*
   Sales channels
Samsung, 128
Sanders, Jerry, 44–45, 152
Segment (entry) barriers, 17, 19–21,
   51, 141, 179–183
Segments: *see* Market segmentation
Semiconductor industry, 2–11,
   15–17, 23, 38–40, 43–44,
   46–47, 50, 59, 63, 65, 76, 77,
   83–84, 86, 102–105, 109, 120,
   122, 127, 128, 132, 134–137,
   158–160, 171, 173
Seminars, 8, 99, 100
Service, 48–49, 53–70, 95, 108
   catching up, 67–68
   corporate leadership and,
      66–67
   costs of good, 69
   customer size and, 64–66
   market segments and, 63–64
   product design and, 57–61
   savings due to good, 68–69
   as strategic problem, 61–63
Shakeout phenomenon, 24
Siemens, 2, 127
Signetics, 84
Silicon compiler, 29

Simplicity
   in product line, 62
   in promotions, 96–98
Soft drink markets, 20
Specialized distributors, 21, 78–81,
   88
Specifications of products, 124
Strategic planning, 175
Strategic principle of marketing,
   12–13, 36, 115, 134, 160
Steel industry, 22
Swatch (watches), 18

Taiwan, 118, 122
Tandem Computer, 20, 138–139
Tektronix, 38, 39
Teletext, 121
Television advertising, 99
Texas Instruments, 2, 3, 84, 112,
   122
Thermco, 128
Toffler, Alvin, 93
Tokyo Electron, 128
Total marketing concept, 156
Townsend, Robert, 2, 4, 90, 94
Trade shows, 99, 127
Transamerica Corporation, 94
Treybig, Jim, 139
Trout, Jack, 91

Underplanning, 145
"Unkunks," 145
Unused products, 84

Vadasz, Les, 3, 134
Valentine, Don, 46
Valid Logic, 115
Videotext, 121

Visicalc, 31
VSLI Technology, Inc. (VTI), 29

Walker, Hap, 54
Wendy's, 96
Winning strategy, 12–36
Word processing software, 40, 41

Xerox, 28, 67

Yawata, K. K., 150–151
Yokagawa Electric Works, 128

Zilog, 3–6, 151

Printed in the United States
By Bookmasters